SATELLITE CASTES *and* DEPENDENT RELATIONS

Dalits in South India

K.E. Rajpramukh

Department of Anthropology
Andhra University

PARTRIDGE
A Penguin Company

Partridge books may be ordered through booksellers or by contacting:

Partridge India
Penguin Books India Pvt.Ltd
11, Community Centre, Panchsheel Park, New Delhi 110017
India
www.partridgepublishing.com
Phone: 000.800.10062.62

ACKNOWLEDGEMENT

There are innumerable studies made on the Caste system in India by scholars of different nationalities, but it is surprising to notice that not a serious study is so far conducted on the dependent relations within the caste system in India. In Andhra Pradesh there are 198 castes and many of them have dependent castes attached to them. In this study, a detailed in-depth investigation is made on a satellite dependent caste of Andhra Pradesh, namely, Mala Masti.

Mala Masti is a satellite dependent caste of the main Mala caste in Andhra Pradesh. In the earlier census reports mention was made of Mala Masti but it was reported that they exist only in three districts in Telangana area. But this study brings to light that they are present in almost all the districts of Andhra Pradesh. The detailed ethnographic account of Mala Masti together with the system of dependent relations which is different from the Jajmani system and Watandari system is brought to light in this study.

This is to acknowledge the contribution of many people who helped in accomplishing the objectives of this project. First of all, I wish to express my gratefulness to the University Grants Commission in liberally funding this project. I wish to place on record our profound gratitude to all those Mala and Mala Masti elders in the study villages without whose cooperation this study would not have been accomplished.

Dr. P.D.S.Palkumar, my former student and later my colleague, conceived the idea of this work and helped in designing the schedules and write up too. The Project Fellow, Dr. K.S.Naidu, painstakingly conducted the field work throughout this study and he has taken meticulous care in the analysis and tabulation of the data. To him goes the credit of putting the materials in place. To both of them I owe my sincere 'Thanks'.

K.E.Rajpramukh

CONTENTS

PREFACE

The Scheduled Castes' (SCs) population in India according to 2011 census is 16.2% of the total Indian population of 1,210,569,573. In Andhra Pradesh State they comprise 16.41% of the total population of 845,80,777. Out of the 59 SCs in the State, Mala, and Madiga, together constitute 90.8% of the SC population of the State. Mala are numerically the second largest group with a population of 5,139,305 (41.6%) after the Madigas, who are numerically the largest (49.2%).

In Andhra Pradesh there are altogether 198 castes and many of these castes have satellite castes attached to them. While sustaining these satellite castes is the responsibility of the main (central) castes, the satellite castes in turn extend a variety of specialized services to their respective main castes and exclusively depend on the main or central castes for their livelihood and sustenance, receiving alms and periodic support from them.

Mala Masti is a satellite dalit (the Government of India's official term is scheduled caste) caste which traditionally depends on the Mala caste for its survival and sustenance. In the earlier census reports mention was made of Mala Masti but it was reported that they exist only in three districts of Telangana (1981 Census Report). But the present study brings to light that they are present in almost all the districts of Andhra Pradesh. It is surprising to notice the paucity of works on such satellite dependent castes in the Indian caste system.

The caste system, as is well known, is founded on structured inequalities that are drawn in to hierarchized and stratified arrangement. It is found that the castes at the bottom too exhibit such a hierarchy. Some earlier studies, especially by Moffat, asserted that the dalits give tacit support to the system but only resent their position in the hierarchy. The bottoms-up approach adopted in earlier studies have not gone beyond this point. These satellite dalit castes, more often than not, are insulted, abused with derogatory terms by the central castes that are themselves much discriminated and excluded from the mainstream. Inequality and exclusion come into sharp focus when the inter-relationships between the central Mala caste and the dependent Mala Masti are analyzed. Such a situation generated much confusion as to their position in the caste hierarchy bringing into focus mutual claims and counter claims for superior position by these castes at the bottom of the system. In such circumstances, the ambiguous position of these dalit satellite castes too contributes to the system's sustenance. The conflicts bordering on much confusion and ambiguity keeps the entire system in tact without being critically questioned by those at the bottom as they are always at loggerheads with other castes at the bottom for a claim of superiority (Rajpramukh and Palkumar, 2009). The study of Mala Masti vis-à-vis the central Mala caste and others in the system would bring to light the nature of dependence relations and the duties and obligations that impinge on such a relationship.

CHAPTER I
INTRODUCTION

Castes in India are ranked endogamous (in-marrying) groups, membership in which is ascribed by birth. There are thousands of castes and sub-castes in India, and each caste is part of a locally based system of interdependence with other groups, involving occupational specialization. They are linked in complex ways with networks that stretch across regions and throughout the nation.

Dalits are at the bottom most rungs of the Caste hierarchy. Most of them live outside the main village in the low-lying areas bordering the fields, and are still socially and physically excluded from many villages. Traditionally they are outside the pale of Hinduism but existentially a part and parcel of the village life. Though, things have changed a little now, the Dalits traditionally were not allowed to come into the villages. They were not allowed to see or meet, talk or touch all other caste people thus everyday experiencing the harshest strictures in the Indian social system.

The existence of rigid ranking is supernaturally validated through the idea of rebirth according to a person's *karma*, the sum of an individual's deeds in this life and in past lives. After death, a person's life is judged by divine forces, and rebirth is assigned into a high or a low place, depending upon what he or she deserved. This supernatural sanction can never be neglected, because it brings a person to his or her position in the caste hierarchy, relevant to every transaction involving food or drink, speaking or touching. In the past, Dalits, especially in parts of south India, had to display extreme deference to high caste people, physically keeping their distance lest their touch or even their shadow should pollute others, wearing neither shoes nor any upper body covering (even for women) in the presence of the upper castes. Dalits, thus, were 'inhumanly' discriminated and traditionally excluded from the whole Indian Society. The Hindu idea of 'pollution' keeps them away from all other castes as they are considered in a state of 'pollution' all the time for ever.

Traditional Position: Dalits were ascribed a peculiar position in the classical Varna system that 'doctrinally they were not part of Hindu Society while existentially they were an integral party of local communities', (Beteille, 1969: 92). In no work on the caste system in India did we find the omission of Dalits and the practice of untouchability. As caste is unique to India it becomes necessary to understand the broad characteristic features of caste system in general before an attempt is made to know the status of Dalits and their satellite castes, and the various dimensions the stigma of untouchability assumes.

Hutton (1946: 49) enumerates the following criteria of caste: (1) Caste is endogamous. (2) There are restrictions on commensality between members of different castes. (3) There is a hierarchical grading of castes, the best recognized position being that of the Brahmin at the top. (4) In various kinds of context, especially those concerned with food, sex and ritual, a member of a 'high' caste is liable to be 'polluted' by either direct or indirect contact with a member of a low caste. (5) Castes are very commonly associated with traditional occupations. (6) A man's caste status is finally determined by the circumstances of his birth, unless he comes to be expelled from his caste for some ritual offence. (7) The system as a whole is always focused around the prestige accorded to the Brahmins.

Ghurye (1961: 1-29) gives six characteristics as fundamental to the caste system. They are (1) Segmental division of society (2) Hierarchy (3) Restrictions on feeding and social intercourse (4) Civil and religious disabilities and privileges of the different sections (5) Lack of unrestricted choice of occupation, and (6) Restrictions on marriage. The disabilities enumerated assume the extreme form only in case of Dalits. Isaac (1965: 28) describes them as "cut out of the community altogether, served and largely still do serve—as its scavengers and sweepers, the handlers of the carcasses of its dead animals whose flesh they eat and whose skins they tan, the carriers of waste and night soil, the beggars and the scrapers, living in and off the dregs and the carrion of the society". For thousands of years they have lived apart, worked apart, eaten apart and even washed apart. Even when they give up their traditional and ritually unclean occupations and take up such respectable roles as cultivators or servants, they continue to suffer the opprobrium and disabilities of their caste status (Harper, 1968: 36). In death and after, the distinction lingers.

In certain areas, besides being untouchable they have been regarded as unapproachable (Sachidananda, 1977: 4). At one place in the South, at one time, the dalits had to keep away from the different levels of upper caste people, 33 feet from the lowest group, 66 feet from the second middle caste group and 99 feet from the Brahmins. Rules ordained that an untouchable had to shout a warning or ring a bell before entering a street so that his contaminating shadow may not fall on the ritually pure persons. What style of dress or ornaments a dalit could wear was also prescribed by custom. He could not enjoy music at weddings, nor could he enter a house belonging to a caste Hindu, or a Hindu temple, or draw water from a common well. Disregard of these prohibitions usually led to serious consequences.

Writing about the low position of these Dalits, Blunt (1969: 336) mentioned that "at all times, the Brahmin Priesthood has endeavored to keep them segregated, not only from Hindu Society, but from the Hindu religion and the Hindu ceremonial; they were not allowed to hear, much less study, the Vedas; they must not enter the temples; they must carry on all ceremonies without using the mantras and no Brahmin would carry out any domestic ceremony for them".

Many diverse and scholarly opinions were given for the lowly status of Dalits. Ambedkar states that the notion of defilement, of pollution and contamination by touch is the basis of untouchability. He (1948:14) mentioned that the prevailing notions of defilement among the Hindus were not different from that which obtained in primitive societies. But there was another form of untouchability observed by Hindus. It was the hereditary untouchability of certain communities. Ambedkar (1948: 21) further stated, "this distinguishes every other system from that of the Hindus—this type of untouchability among Hindus stands in a class by itself . . . they are born impure, they are impure while they live, they have the death of the impure and they give birth to children who are born with the stigma of untouchability affixed to them".

Writing about the Indian Caste hierarchy, Stevenson (1954: 46-57) makes a distinction between ritual status and social status. In case of Dalits, apart from their low ritual status, their social status is also low. Srinivas (1956: 73-96), stated that 'untouchability is more than ritual rank and the pollution it carries; there is a congruence of economic, ritual and political statuses in the case of Dalits'. For them the correlation between caste and occupation, ritual and social status has been a rigid one in the past. Beteille (1969: 93) also agreed with Srinivas by stating that the low rank of the Dalits was derived from the cumulative inequalities in the economic, political and ritual spheres".

The Hindu philosophical concepts of *Karma* (fate) and *Dharma* (duty), with the cultural sanction, have been integrally connected with untouchability. Failure to perform one's *'Dharma'* in the previous birth is given as the reason for one's birth as an untouchable; belief in *Karma* led to its corollary of low birth being associated with one's failure to perform one's *Dharma.* Conversely birth in a high caste meant acting according to one's *Dharma* in past life.

Purity and Pollution: The status differences in Indian society are expressed in terms of ritual purity and pollution. Notions of purity and pollution are extremely complex and vary greatly in different regions among different castes and religious groups. However, broadly speaking, high status is associated with purity and low status with pollution. Some kinds of purity are inherent, or inborn; for example, gold is purer than copper by its very nature, and similarly, a member of a high-ranking

Brahman or priestly caste is born with more inherent purity than a member of a low-ranking sweeper caste.

Ritual cleanliness also determines purity—daily bathing in flowing water, dressing in properly laundered clothes of approved materials, eating only the foods appropriate for one's caste, refraining from physical contact with people of lower rank, and avoiding involvement with ritually impure substances. The latter include body wastes and excretions, most especially those of another adult person. Contact with the products of death or violence are typically polluting and threatening to ritual purity.

For Hutton (1946:49), the 'pollution' concept governs the mutual relationships of the castes and it also results in caste exclusiveness ascribing a distinct status for each caste group. In this context, Dumont and Pocock (1961: 34) point out that "the fear of pollution governs social relations and that hereditary specialization, hierarchical organization and reciprocal repulsion lend uniqueness to the caste system". Nevertheless, the extreme form of pollution can be seen only in case of Dalits who were treated as untouchables by the rest of the castes.

An enormous body of scholarly work exists on the Indian system of castes. For Dumont (1980), Indian society is basically defined by the hierarchy of castes. Caste "is above all, a system of ideas and values, a formal comprehensible rational system . . . [imbued with] the idea of hierarchy". "Purity" and "pollution" remain central to the caste system—indeed, central to Hinduism itself—and for the Brahmin purification and hygiene are a necessity (Dumont, 1980: 52).

This argument is opposed among others by Dipankar Gupta, who argues that Dumont's idea oversimplifies caste and papers over regional particularities and transactions.

"It is impossible to construct a uniform hierarchy of caste based on the notion of purity and pollution. No caste would acquiesce to its placement among the so-called "untouchables." No caste would agree that members of other castes are made up of substances better than theirs. No caste would like its people to marry outside the community. No caste would like to merge its identity with any other caste. No caste accepts that it has originated from a shameful act of miscegenation. Any suggestion of being half-breed is dismissed haughtily across the board by all castes" (Gupta, 2000: 33).

Caste-Occupation linkage: Caste basically is linked to production and occupation. It is a system of division of labour from which the element of competition has been largely excluded. "Economic roles are allocated by right to closed minority groups of low social status; members of the high status 'dominant caste' to whom the low status groups are bound, generally form a numerical majority and must compete among themselves for the services of individual members of the lower castes" (Leach, 1960: 5-6).

In the pre-British period under the *Jajmani* system, the blacksmith, carpenter, potter, oilman, barber, washer-man, and priest all became linked with the household of the upper caste landowner and were paid in kind by the landholder for services rendered during the year. This arrangement helped to ensure the durability of the caste system in the rural countryside (Srinivas, 1962; Leach, 1960). When the principle of heredity is added to this, caste soon solidified into a family trade as well as an almost irreversible social category that was maintained as much by social taboo as by economic imperative.

Thus the dalit, who is outside the pale of the caste system is trapped by his own economic trade. The dalit's lowly status begins with the untouchable castes becoming associated with those groups specializing in 'impure' tasks, such as scavenging, skinning cattle, working on leather, butchery, and supervising cremations. Leather workers, washer-men, scavengers, undertakers of toilet cleaning, toddy-tapers, sweepers and rural laborers were polluted because of their work. Their role in the caste-based economic system meant that the modern dalits, descended from the professionals of impure tasks, are heirs to centuries old filth, professional as well as psychological.

Hierarchy among the Dalits: In an attempt to closely examine the contention of Moffatt that the principle of hierarchy operates among the dalits as strongly as at the top, Sudhakara Rao (2001) identified three important principles especially among the Dalits in claiming superior status. The first principle is 'proximity with high castes and services'. "The principle of association ranks the groups within the village just as it ranks individuals within the group. Proximity to high caste people, which equals economic and political centrality, certainly provides an untouchable with higher status. This principle of hierarchy among untouchables can be found if social distance in every day social intercourse is analyzed" (Sudhakara Rao, 2001:84).

The second principle operating behind the hierarchy among the untouchable castes is incorporation in the ritual and reception of temple 'honours' of the high castes. In Tamil Nadu, as Appadurai and Beckenridge (1976) and Dirks (1987) have shown, *thozihil* associated with temples are fundamental to social order and hierarchy.

The third principal in structuring untouchable castes lies in the imitation of political and economic role relationship of the local dominant caste by the other castes. Moffatt recognizes the fact that the dalits replicated the domination of politically and economically influential families in Endavur Reddiyars, in response to their specific exclusion (Moffatt 1975: 91). But he assumes that the replication of domination took place to the extent that the dominant untouchable caste created and maintained a hierarchy within the untouchable castes to exclude the 'impure'. But one can also find replication of paternalistic relations of the dominant caste emerging out of the political and economic power rather than the religious values and exclusion of 'impure'.

"The political power, as Fuller (1977) argued, was brought about in India by numerical strength and control of land. Wherever a group consolidated its numerical strength and occupied land, it generated a territorial social organization in which hierarchical relations were manifested. The dominant caste, clan or lineage that controlled a large extent of a land and labour produced inequality and created hierarchical relations with the less dominant or numerically weak clan or lineage or sub-caste and other castes, and developed mechanisms to reproduce those hierarchical relations (see Dirks 1987). Therefore, we find uneven territorial distribution of different caste groups, predominance of certain caste people in one area and some other caste in another area. This, of course, is an over-simplification of the complex social formation where political, economic and religious matters are inextricably interwoven, but it captures the idea of caste domination in space and time. Several subordinate and dependent castes gathered around such dominant castes over a period of time; it could be otherwise also, but the fact remains that the existence of a dominant caste in an area and a village has been a common phenomenon in the country. Dirks' (1987) study describes the rising up of such a dominant tribe or caste to royal status" (Sudhakara Rao, 2001:89-90).

Studies on Dalits: Many volumes on 'Castes and Tribes in India' and works on Indian Village Communities have brought to light the position of Dalits and mention may be made of Crooke (1896), Thurston (1909), Ketkar (1909), Iyer (1909), Risley (1915), Ibbetson (1916), Senart (1930), Blunt (1931), Hutton (1946), Mckim Marriot (1955), Bailey (1957), Mayer (1960), Ghurye (1961), Chauhan (1967), Sita Deulkar (2004), Pathak and Pandey (2005), and Thorat, (2009).

Works on individual Dalit castes are very few in number. One of the earliest full-length monographs on one of the Dalits was 'The Chamar' by Briggs (1920). It dealt with the social aspects of the *Chamar* and their beliefs and practices. The monograph was descriptive in nature and gives a static picture of the *Chamars*. The aspect of change was not dealt with. No attempt was made to discern any social mobility among them. The author who was a Christian missionary, concluded that Christianity offered to the *Chamar* a satisfactory place in the social order and a satisfactory religious life and that it was only in Christianity that there was a real hope of redemption for them.

Stephen Fuchs' (1949), 'The Children of Hari' was a full length monograph of all aspects of the life of the *Balahis,* a Dalit caste, in the Nimar district of Madhya Pradesh. Singh (1969) has made a full-length study of the social structure and change among the *Madigas,* a Dalit caste, in Andhra Pradesh. The study described the current changes affecting the *Madiga,* the secular order of society and spread of egalitarian values in the wake of the constitutional privileges. He has noticed that while the distance between the high castes and the *Madigas* has narrowed, the gulf between them and the other Dalits increased.

The processes of sanskritization and westernization, the reform movements and the constitutional privileges were presented as the major causative factors of social change in the various village studies that appeared in the post-independence period. Many of the village studies contain detailed accounts of a number of Dalit castes under the aspect of change. Beteille (1966) detailed the relationship between the Brahmin, the non-Brahmin, the *Adi-Dravid* and the untouchable castes (*Paraiya* and *Palla*) in a village of Tamilnadu. He showed how caste system overlapped the class structure to a large extent, although certain aspects of life such as land ownership, occupation etc., were not dependent upon caste as before. Epstein (1962) revealed in her study of two villages in Mysore that the provision of the reserved seats for the Dalits on the village *panchayat* did not mean real power for them as they were still dependent on their peasant masters. Unless the democratic legislation was accompanied by redistribution of land in favour of the Dalits it remains ineffective. The Dalits were competing among themselves and thus their unity was impaired. Unless there was a change in the production relationships, the social legislation in favour of the Dalits would remain a dead letter. Harper (1968) made a study of the Dalits, the *Holeru* caste in Mysore. The Holeru tried to gain prestige by assuming behavioural patterns associated with higher castes, such as refusal to perform such tasks that were ritually degrading. All these studies point to certain changes affecting the lives of the Dalits, but they did not definitely indicate that these changes resulted in the upward social mobility of the Dalits.

Different approaches to the study of caste system: Of late, there were attempts to study the caste system from the point of view of dalits adopting an approach called 'bottoms-up'. In his study of a South Indian Dalit community, Michael Moffat (1979) argues that the untouchables live in consensus with the wider Indian culture by replicating among themselves virtually every relation and institution from which they have been excluded by the higher castes. Moffat's is a significant contribution in pointing out that the Dalits accord tacit allegiance to the system as a whole but they only resent their relative position in the caste hierarchy. But Mendelsohn and Vicziany (1998) refute Moffat's claim that untouchables are no different from caste Hindus and buy into the very ideology of purity and pollution that stigmatizes them. In addition to their own studies that reveal untouchable distinctiveness, counter-culture, and resistance, they draw on older studies, such as those by Gough and Mencher. Some more recent studies that support their argument include that of L. Vincentnathan (1987, 1993a, 1994b), S. G. Vincentnathan (1996), Deliège (1994, 1996), and Mosse (1994).

Deliege (1992) closely examines Moffatt's arguments and, in particular, the relationship between `replication' and `consensus', Moffatt's key concepts. He strongly contends that there is no necessary link between them.

Furthermore, even though untouchables may make references to caste ideology to explain the inferiority of the castes below them, they do not accept their own position within the system.

The most startling and complex argument Mendelsohn and Vicziany (1998) make is that the Indian government itself contributes to the oppression and continued poverty of untouchables. Instead of seeing anomalous and isolated cases of government oppression—such as scattered cases of police brutality and complicity in violence against untouchables, or discrimination by a few misguided bureaucrats—the authors suggest that government abuse and indifference is endemic. This is especially so, as the government is largely controlled by the upper castes.

Inter-dependence and inter-relations of castes in Indian villages have been brought to light by several studies. Every caste by necessity enters into several forms of relationship in the social, economic, political and ritual spheres. Interdependence, as a characteristic feature of caste has been well explored. However, the dependence relations between satellite castes, which rely entirely on their main castes, are not studied intensively. Especially such dependence relations among the Dalit castes did not receive proper attention from scholars interested in the study of caste system. Besides, the ethnographic details of the satellite castes have not been fully explored.

Objectives of the Study: In this background this study was undertaken with the following objectives:

1. To establish the fact that Mala Masti are present in almost all the Districts of Andhra Pradesh

2. To study the origin, socio-economic status and rites-de-passage of Mala Masti

3. To explore the nature of the Mala Masti dependence relations with the Malas; and

4. To examine how recent changes are affecting the satellite castes.

Methodology: The study in the first place ascertained the presence of the Mala Masti in different districts by means of a Survey. Subsequently the study covered a dozen districts in Andhra Pradesh by making an in-depth study of Mala Masti in randomly selected villages. In order to accomplish the above cited objectives a well prepared census schedule and the household schedule were administered to the Mala Masti respondents in the villages selected. The household schedule was pre-tested and a few case studies were also collected. In addition a few elaborate informal interviews were conducted on the Mala and Mala Masti elders in all the villages studied. The fieldwork was conducted during 2009 and 2010.

CHAPTER II
MALA AND MADIGA: THE MAIN OR CENTRAL CASTES

Mala and Madiga are the two prominent Dalit castes in Andhra Pradesh. Though the official word, 'Scheduled Castes' include 59 castes, the word Dalit refers mainly to these two castes. Traditionally the Malas are the agricultural labourers although in some parts they are also weavers, and the Madigas are leather workers. The performance of certain indispensable social, economic and ceremonial tasks integrates them with the village and its life. The corresponding castes in some other States are Palla, Paraiya (Tamilnadu), Cheruman, Pulayan (Kerala), Holeya, Madiga (Karnataka), Mahar, Mang (Maharashtra), Bhangi, Chamar (Bihar, Punjab) etc. Hardly a village in Andhra is seen without the two hamlets of Malas and Madigas.

Nomenclature: Until 1931, in the decennial Census Reports, these untouchable castes were placed under the category of depressed classes. But some of these untouchables sought a new name as a means of achieving superior status by erasing the blot and stigma attached to their traditional caste names. Ambedkar in a supplementary memorandum submitted to the round table conference (in November, 1931) on the claims of the depressed castes for special representation stated:

"In dealing with this part of the question we would like to point out that the existing nomenclature of the depressed classes who have given thought to it . . . it is degrading and contemptuous and advantage might be taken of this occasion for drafting the new constitution to alter for official purposes the existing nomenclature. We think they should be called 'non-caste Hindus', 'protestant Hindus' or 'non-conformist Hindus' or some such designation". From such an atmosphere sprang up a crop of names distorting the real identity of several castes.

The position given to the depressed classes in census reports is exhaustively reviewed by Reddy (1952: 43-59). The Commissioner of Indian Census, 1931, on the suggestion of the Superintendent of Assam Census preferred the term 'Exterior Castes' to the label 'Depressed Castes'. Mr. Yeats, the Census Superintendent of Madras, vehemently protested at that time against this change of label. Against this, in the report of the Census of India, Hutton argued that the term 'exterior' might connote exclusion but not extrusion. However the term 'exterior' was used for all practical purposes of Census operations.

With the passage of Government of India Act, 1935, they have been consistently referred to as 'Scheduled Castes'. The expression thus standardized in the Indian Constitution was first coined by the Simon Commission and embodied in the Section 309 of the Government of India Act, 1935. The Census of India, 1941, following this schedule changed the term 'Exterior Castes' to 'Scheduled Castes'. After the Indian National Congress took over the administration in 1946, preceding the independence of the country, the generic term scheduled caste is generally used in official usage in favour of the Gandhian epithet "the Harijan". The latest term 'Dalit' came into existence in the early 60s with the emergence of Dalit Panthers in Maharashtra.

The Dalits: The term 'Dalit' has roots in Sanskrit where the root 'dal' means 'to split, crack, open'. This Indo-European root appears in German and English in the form of 'dal' or *'tal'*, meaning 'cut'. In English, 'dale' is a valley, a cut in the ground; in German, *'thal'*: a tailor is one who cuts; 'to tell a tale' is the same as 'to cut a tally', the cut-marks made by the shepherd on his staff when counting sheep.

'Dalit' has come to mean things or persons who are cut, split, broken or torn asunder, scattered or crushed and destroyed. By coincidence, in Hebrew language there is a root 'dal' meaning low, weak, or poor. In the Bible, different forms of this term have been used to describe people who have been reduced to nothingness or helplessness. The present usage of the term Dalit goes back to the nineteenth century, when a Marathi social reformer and revolutionary, Mahatma Jyotirao Phule (1826-1890), used it to describe the outcastes and untouchables as the oppressed and the broken victims of the caste-ridden society. Under the charismatic leadership of Dr. B.R. Ambedkar (1891-1956), this term gained greater importance and popularity. During the 1970s, the followers of the Dalit Panther Movement of Maharastra gave currency to the term 'Dalit' as a constant reminder of their age-old oppression, denoting both their state of deprivation and the people who are oppressed. This term for them is not a mere name or title: for them it has become an expression of hope, the hope of recovering their past self-identity. The term has gained a new connotation with a more positive meaning. It must be remembered that *Dalit does not mean Caste or low-Caste or poor;* it refers to the deplorable state or condition to which a large group of people has been reduced by social convention and in which they are placed at the bottom.

Malas and Madigas: The report of the Indian Census 1901, describes the Mala, and Madiga as castes, "who eat beef and pollute even without touch". In the Censuses of 1901 and 1911, the two castes returned themselves without any change in nomenclature. But by 1921, some events happened to affect the returns, as the Superintendent of Madras Census, Boag (1922: 158) evidences:

". . . the castes commonly known as the "depressed classes" . . . have come into prominence recently partly by reason of their assertion of equal rights of humanity and citizenship with members of the superior castes, partly owing to industrial disputes with members of superior castes which led to serious riots and disturbances in Madras, and partly owing to the measures taken by the Government in recent years to improve their conditions. Following the established practice, their first move in the direction of social advancement has been an agitation for a change of name; but they are not all of one opinion as to the most desirable name, some favour Adi-Dravida for the Tamils and Adi-Andhra for the Telugus, others favour Dravida".

In the same report Boag observed that the vast majority of them continued to stand for their traditional caste names. Only a few of them returned themselves under the new nomenclature. In the 1931 Census the two untouchable castes of Andhra, Mala and Madiga, figured under several labels such as Adi-Andhra, Adi—Dravida, Chandala, Jambavulu, Maila in the Census tables. The state of untouchability has been taken as the criterion for classification under exterior castes. The Superintendent of Madras Census 1931, Yeats writes: "Among the many circumstances that go to produce the depressed state, untouchability is prominent, and it was decided that for the purposes of this Census allocation to this category should follow this criterion".

Origin of Mala and Madiga Castes: Stuart stated that, "the Malas are the Pariahs of the Telugu country" (Thurston, 1975: 329). It is worth noting that in the vedas the root 'mla' meant to 'tan'. This suggests that Mala also worked on leather (Ghurye, 1961: 228). Dr. Oppert derives the word 'Mala' from a Dravidian root, meaning a mountain, which is represented by the Tamil Malai, Telugu Mala, etc., so that Mala is the equivalent of Paraiya, and also of Mar or Mhar and the Mal of Western and Central Bengal (Hutton, 1975: 329-33). In C.P. Brown's Telugu Dictionary, it is derived from 'maila' which means dirty. According to mythology prevailing in various parts of Andhra Pradesh, Malas and Madigas claim origin from two watchmen who were with Lord Siva. The myth runs thus: Lord Siva and his wife goddess Parvathi possessed a beautiful cow called Kamadhenu which used to give milk whenever it is needed, and to look after it two boys were appointed. Never once they were given the milk of the cow. But one day, it so happened that Parvathi quite inadvertently gave the remnants of boiled milk in a pot, to one of the boys. He found it to be very tasty and thought the meat of the cow would be tastier. He instigated the other boy to kill the cow and they both ate the meat.

Knowing this ghastly act, Lord Siva cursed them to be born as Untouchables. Accordingly the boy who incited the other to kill the cow was called 'Mala' and the one who actually killed it was called as 'Madiga'.

Singh (1969: 4-5) gave a little modified version. He writes that only one boy called Chennayya was appointed to look after the cow. When this boy asked for some milk, Parvathi directed him to the cow and ask for it. The moment he did this, the cow fell on the ground and died. To feast on it's flesh, the gods requisitioned the services of Jambavant who was senior most among the gods and was born six months before the creation of the earth. Siva ordered Chennayya to call Jambavant who was performing penance. Obeying Siva the boy said to Jambavant, "Tata maha digira" (grandfather come down). The old man came down. He lifted the carcass with his left hand, and carried it to a convenient spot where the Gods could cut and skin it. The gods wanted Jambavanta to put the flesh in two heaps, one for eating and the other for bringing the cow back to life with *mantras*. Jambavanta put all the flesh in one pot and lighted a fire under it. While stirring, a piece of flesh fell down on the ground. Chennayya, picked it up, cleaned it and put it again in the pot. Siva and other gods were angry with Jambavanta as he had not divided the meat into two parts so as to bring the cow back to life from one of the two parts. They were also annoyed with Chennayya for having put the piece, fallen in the dust back into the pot. They cursed both Jambavanta and Chennayya: to lead a degraded life in *Kaliyugam* (The fourth and final age in the cyclic order of time—according to Hindu belief) by earning their livelihood through handling dead cattle and sweeping village lanes. Jambavanta and Chennayya ate the flesh and drank the liquor. Jambavanta took the cow hide and gave it to his sons: they became leather workers. Chennayya's descendants took to cleaning village lanes. Jambavanta's descendants are the Madigas and Chennayya's descendants are the Malas.

According to Singh (1969: 4) in Telangana, it is held that Jambavanta, the mythological ancestor of Madigas came down to help when he was summoned by them with the following words: "*Tata, Maha digi ra*" (Great Grand Father, come down). From then onwards he was also known as 'Mahadige'—'the great man who came down'. His descendants were called '*maha dige waru*': which was later on corrupted into Madiga. The same version is in vogue in Andhra also.

Singh gives another explanation connecting the caste name to the groups' practice of accepting carrion as an item of food. He writes: "When cattle died, the ancestors of the Madiga claimed them with the assertion '*madigoddu*' which means that 'the cattle is mine'. Thus they came to be called *madigoddu*. Thus,"madigoddu" was corrupted as *madigodu* and evntually it became Madiga" (1969: 4).

In Southern India all the castes are divided into right hand and left hand divisions. Hutton states that this curious tradition is only found in Southern India by which certain castes are regarded as castes of the right hand and others as castes of left hand (1946: 67). He further states that the inhabitants of the Andhra country appear to be more volatile and temperamental than their neighbours, and in particular, are noted for the outbreaks or rioting between the castes of the right hand and of the left, two ancient factions in which the low castes of Mala and Madiga are respectively prominent as protagonists (1946: 67). The traditional rivalry between these two castes is reported in many works.

"Between these two divisions there is a very strong sentiment of faction rivalry, leading to frequent clashes, often with riot and violence, generally occasioned by some real or supposed encroachment by castes of the left hand on privileges as belonging exclusively to the right" (Hutton, 1946:11 and 167) traces the origin of society into two groups, castes of the right hand and castes of the left hand from a system of inheritance prevailing in Telugu, Kanarese and Tamil countries long ago.

There are different versions as to how the Malas are included in the right hand section while the Madigas occupied the left hand section. In this connection, Thurston (1909: 315-316) writes: "At a remote period, *Jambava* Rishi, a sage, was questioned by *Iswara* (Siva), why the former was habitually late at the Divine Court. The Rishi replied that he had to attend personally to the wants of children every day, which consequently made his attendance late; where upon Iswara, pitying the children, gave the Rishi a cow (*Kamadhenu*), which instantaneously supplied their every want. Once upon a time while Jambava was at Iswara's court, another Rishi named Sankya, visited Jambava's hermitage, where he was hospitably entertained by his son Yugamuni".

To summarize Thurston's version, Sankya was tempted to taste the cow's flesh after eating the extremely delicious cream made from Kamadhenu's milk. Yugamuni refused to kill the divine animal when he was induced to do so by Sankya. Sankya killed the cow himself and prevailed upon Yugamuni to partake of the flesh. On his return from Iswara's court Jambava found the inmates of his hermitage eating the flesh of the sacred cow. He took both Sankya and Yugamuni to Iswara for judgement. Instead of entering into the court the two offenders remained outside, Sankya

Rishi, standing on the right side, and Yugamuni, on the left side of the doorway. Iswara cursed them to become *Chandals* or outcastes. Sankyas descendants came to be known as Holeya (corresponding to the Malas of Andhra) and Yugamuni's as Madiga. Since Sankya stood on the right side of the doorway at Iswara's court, Holeyas are the right hand caste whereas Madiga are known as the left hand caste by virtue of their ancestor standing on the left side of Iswara's court.

A different version was given by Singh (1969: 5-6):"*Jambavant* was the king of *Jambudweepam*. He was the owner of a Divine cow, the like of which no other king of the day was privileged to own. The Divine cow had the unique powers of granting any wish of the owner if he prayed to her. A neighbouring king was visiting Jambavant. To extend hospitality to his royal guest, worthy of one great king to another, Jambavant prayed to the divine cow to anticipate and fulfill the wishes of the visitor. To the astonishment of the guest, the very instant there came forth almost everything he could desire. The king was very much impressed by the powers of the Divine cow. He requested Jambavant to give away the cow to him, but the latter, after consulting his sons, declined. The king felt insulted, and ordered his men to capture the cow. The king's men attacked Jambavant's palace, and in the battle that ensued the king was defeated. After sometime the defeated king once again attacked Jambavant's palace, but this time the Divine cow cursed him, and he was burnt to ashes. The king's son was enraged and was determined to take revenge on Jambavant. Dressed as a poor man, he entered the palace in Jambavant's absence and induced the latter's son to kill the cow so that he could feast on her flesh. On knowing this Jambavant took the offenders to the court of Siva for judgment. Fearing the wrath of Siva the two offenders did not enter the court: they stood outside by the two sides of the doorway. Siva cursed them to become *Chandal* or Untouchable. The one who stood on the right hand side of the door way became the ancestor of the Mala caste, while the one who was on the left became the ancestor of the Madiga" (1969: 5-6)

The distinction between the right and left hand castes become clearer with respect to the claims they lay on certain privileges that are denied to the other group. Ghurye (1961: 12-13) writes in this regard quoting Madras Census Report (1871: 129) that: "The right hand castes claim certain privileges which they strongly refuse to those of the left hand, viz., riding on horse-back in processions, carrying *standars* with certain devices, and supporting their marriage booths on twelve pillars. They insist that the left hand castes must not raise more than eleven pillars to the booth nor employ their standard devices peculiar to the right hand castes".

Traditional Status: The origin of caste system is in *varnashrama* Dharma, the division of society into four Varnas Viz., Brahmin, Kshatriya, Vaisya and Sudra. The first three Varnas are twice-born (*dwija*), the first birth being from the mother and the second from the investiture with the sacred girdle which is denied to the Sudras. Therefore the first three Varnas are born twice while the Sudra is born only once (Manu Smrithi, Ch.XI, Verse 4). Among the four Varnas each preceding Varna is superior by birth to the one following. It is popularly held that in the beginning there were only three varnas and the fourth varna of the Sudra is an outcome of the fight between

Brahmins and Kshtriya for the supremacy in the Varna hierarchy.

Sudras were divided into *'byojyanna'* (food prepared by them is partaken by Brahmins) and *'abhojyannas'* (food prepared by them is not partaken by Brahmins). The first includes owned slaves (Kane, 1974: 121-22). Historically untouchables were treated as *'abhojyanna'* and therefore were not the slaves or domestic servants in ancient India. Those Sudras who were called *Chandalas, Asprisyas, Nishadas, Vartyas* are out of the Varna system. They lived outside the main settlements. These castes are also known as 'avarnas' meaning thereby that they do not belong to any 'varna'.

There was no fifth Varna in the earlier Smrithis, but untouchables were referred to as Panchamas (Kane, 1974: 168). Dasus or Dasyus were non-Aryans and did not belong to the Varnas. Hence they were treated as Avarnas. They were opposed to Varna system and did not follow Brahminic ceremonies (Das, in Ambedkar, 1946: 104), They were conquered and gradually made slaves (Kane, 1974: 73). The term Sudra is derived from the root words, Shue (sorrow) and Dru (overcome), which means that one who has overcome sorrow (Kane, 1974: 155).

Writing about the origin of the practice of untouchability, Ghurye (1961: 214) states: "Ideas of purity, whether occupational or ceremonial which are found to have been a factor in the genesis of caste are the very soul of the idea and practice of untouchability. The fact that in the sacrificial creation of mankind the last order mentioned as having been created from the feet of the creator is that of the Sudra and that there was no other class of human beings created thereafter, adds flesh and blood to the ideas of ceremonial and occupational purity to engender the theory and practice of untouchability."

In the *Rigveda,* three classes of society are very frequently mentioned and named Brahma, Kshatra, and Vis. The first two represented broadly the two professions of the Poet-Priest and the Warrior-Chief. The third division was apparently a group comprising all the common people. "It is only in one of the later hymns, the celebrated *Purushasukta,* that a reference has been made to four orders of society as emanating from the sacrifice of the Primeval Being. The names of those four orders are given there as Brahmana, Rajanya, Vaisya and Sudra, who are said to have come respectively from the mouth, the arms, the thighs and the feet of the creator. The particular limbs associated with these divisions and the order in which they are mentioned probably indicate their status in the society of the time, though no such interpretation is directly given in the hymn" (Ghurye, 1961: 43).

Hutton (1963: 149) writes about the occupational division among these four Varnas thus: "To the Brahmans were assigned divinity and the six duties of studying, teaching, sacrificing, assisting others to sacrifice, giving alms and receiving gifts to the end that the Vedas might be protected; the Kshatriya were assigned strength and duties of studying, sacrificing, giving alms using weapons, protecting treasure and life, to the end that good government should be assured; to the Vaishya were allotted the power of work and the duties of studying and tending cattle, to the end that Labour should be productive; and to the Sudra was given the duty of serving the three higher Varna."

In the Vedic literature the untouchables were referred to as Chandalas. About them, Ghurye (1961:216) writes:

"The *Dharmasutra* writers declare the Chandalas to be the progeny of the most hated of the reverse order of mixed unions, that of a Brahmin female with a Sudra male".

This has been considered as an extreme of *'pratiloma'* and thus the Chandalas were degraded to a position of untouchability far inferior to the other categories of *pratiloma* which is a reverse order of marriage, where a high caste or varna woman marries a low caste or Varna man. Hutton (1963: 207) opined that the origin of the position of the exterior (untouchable) castes is partly racial, partly religious, and partly a matter of social custom. There are historical accounts also about the origin of untouchables. Isaacs (1965: 30-31) writes about the origin of untouchables thus:

"The most commonly repeated version is that it all dates back to prehistoric times, perhaps four or five thousand years ago, when otherwise unidentified 'Aryan' invaders made themselves the masters of the indigenous population they found in that dim time came, it is alleged, the relationship between upper and lower castes in India today, with the Shudras associated with the subjugated people of that prehistoric time, and the Untouchables with some lower than low separation that was made at the bottom of the social scale. There is a matter of skin colour involved here also although it, too, like everything else, has been lowered through time, ignorance, and controversy. The word 'Varna' or 'Caste' actually means 'colour' and it has often been said that the 'Arya' were fair in complexion and the 'Dasa' or 'Dasyus', the local people, were 'dark'. In Vedic times up to about 600 B.C. the authorities say, the conquered people were called 'the dark people'. The Dravidian people of southern India were, and still largely are, a black or dark people, and these differences are the sources of a sometimes—virulent modern 'Aryansim' among some Indians. In any case the protective system of exclusions and separations for the Brahmins and other upper castes presumably began as a way of solidifying and maintaining power over a conquered mass and there is some suggestion that the first untouchable groups emerged from forbidden and strongly tabooed mixing between the high and the low. It seems likely enough that the 'purity' the Brahmins tried to maintain was not merely ritual and not only political but racial".

The Untouchables had to submit themselves to the shackles of traditional doctrines, as they were helpless in social, economic and religions spheres of life. They were treated as slaves and disobedience results in social ostracism. Isaacs (1965: 28) described them thus: "The untouchables, cut out of the community altogether, served—and largely still do serve—as its scavengers and sweepers, the handlers of the carcasses of its dead animals whose flesh they eat and whose skin they tan, the carriers, of waste and night soil, the beggars and the scrapers living in and off the dregs and carrion of the society. Besides this they perform a good part of the plain ordinary toil of the fields".

They were not allowed to enter the temples to draw water from the public wells, to use any public transportation: and even to change their occupation. Above all, their touch was considered defiling and in some places even their shadow also defiling. Such was the position of the Indian untouchables in the traditional Hindu Society. The untouchables of the Andhra, the Mala and Madiga, were no exception for this malady. Traditionally the Malas are agricultural labourers and in some parts weaving also is considered as their traditional occupation. The traditional occupation of Madigas is working on leather. The Malas and Madigas are integrated into the village economy because of their traditional occupation of menial service, scavenging, leatherwork, drum-beating etc. Besides, the Mala and Madiga had to perform certain ritual duties in times of marriages, festivals and other social occasions.

From the knowledgeable informants who remember the days of their grandfathers and great grandfathers, it is learnt that the Malas and Madigas were treated as dregs of the society and the strictures imposed against them were harsh and inhuman. They were not allowed to use the main streets of the village. Their touch was considered to be polluting. Their occupations were considered to be defiling. They were not allowed to wear the same dress of the high caste Hindus. They were not allowed to use *chappals* (foot-wear) or umbrellas. When they enter the village they had to carry their *chappals* in hands and to fold their umbrellas. Even the possession of such materials like footwear, umbrella etc., evokes the wrath of the high caste landowners. Men covered their loins with coarse cloth and above waist they were prohibited to wear anything. Women wear *sarees* exposing the portion below the knees. They were not allowed to wear blouses; they used to tie a small spittoon round their neck so that they had to spit into that only. They were not allowed to spit on the ground, which was considered to be defiling. They had to give way by standing far away from the road, to a high caste man who is passing through that way. They were not allowed to enter the front yard of the high caste man's house. They had to talk to him only from the backyard of the house.

CHAPTER III
THE DEPENDENT CASTES

The dependent castes are referred to as satellite castes by some scholars (Singh, T.R, 1969; Raju, M.V.T, 1980). But this term, satellite castes, implies more than economic dependence. Writing about the Madigas, Singh (1969:31) states, ". . . . here the main supporting caste has been called the *central caste*; the others economically dependent upon, but complementing the socio-cultural life of the former, have been *satellite castes*". Raju (1980) believed that this system is an extension of *'Watandari'* system in which the servant-master relationships are well defined. But in case of dependent castes the socio-cultural relations are predominant more than the economic relations that characterize the *watandari* system. In this study the terms "main" and "central" are interchangeably used with the same meaning. In the same way, "dependent castes" and "satellite castes" are used with the same meaning.

***Watandari, Jajmani* and the Dependent Caste Systems:**
Watandari system was in vogue in Telangana. *'Watan'* is a urdu word which means land, birth place with alternative meanings of land that was given as hereditary right or authority. Accordingly, *'Watandar'* means the one appointed by the Government in a village to perform the assigned duties and who was given the village land as

'inaam' (gift) in lieu of his services, by the Government. He thus received all the *fruits* of the land. Watandari system was thus related to Village administration/ governance. When Asafjahi dynasti was ruling Telangana, Salar Jung, the Prime-Minister (1853-1883) introduced many reforms and one such was the *'Watandari'* system. Entire village administration depended on this system in which there used to be 15 *Watandars* in the village. They were of two types: Village Officers and Village Servants. Village Officers were three in number: Village Accountant (*Karanam*), Police Patel and Maali Patel. The twelve Village servants were: shaik sindhi or majkuri, neerudi, talaari (these three keep a watch on the village), purohith, vadrangi, kanchari, kummari, mangali, chakali, begari, dappu madiga, and vetti madiga. It may be noted here that 'begari' is from Mala caste who attends to serve the visiting officials. Both vetti Madiga and begari offer various services to the officials. Vetti refers to their services in disposing of the dead bodies in burial or cremation. For their services they get a small amount of money as salary in addition to performing in different festivals for which they receive *'balootha'*(gift) in the form of grain from the villagers. For this reason all the twelve *watandars* are called *'baloothedars'*. Their office was hereditary although the Government has the right to remove them from office any time. This system was abolished in 1977 by the Andhra Pradesh Government.

The *jajmani* system is different in that the different occupational groups within a village such as blacksmith, carpenter, barber, washer-man, potter, weaver, leather worker, offer their specialized services to the land owners that are indispensable for an agrarian economy. Those who receive such services are called *'jajmans'* and who serve them are the 'kamins'. For their services the kamins get paid in cash and kind which is usually a quantum of grain paid annually at the harvest time. These *jajman-kamin* relations bind families through generations. Thus the cultivators depend on all the service rendering castes within a village. As such, from the priest to the leather worker all the service rendering castes participate in all the rituals of the *Jajman*.

Similarities and differences of these systems:

1. Watandari system was established by the Government whereas Jajmani system and 'Dependent caste system' were not appointed by Government. The former includes all the castes in the village where as in the later the relationships are between the *jajman* and *kamin* only, and in dependent system between the main caste and the satellite castes.

2. In Watandari system the salaries and *inaams* (gifts) are from the Government which appoints different *watans*. In Jajmani system and in Dependent system the relationships are established by the land owners and different castes. Continuation or dissolution of such arrangements depends on the respective land owners only.

3. In all the three systems hereditary rights have a place but with a difference. In Watandari system the *'inaam* land' given by the Government is a permanent arrangement. In the Jajmani system, the

'miraasi' is according to the agreement between the *jajman* and the *kamin*. In the 'dependent system' the payments or alms are determined by the satisfaction and happiness the 'patron' derives from the acts of the dependent satellite caste. Even if the main caste fails to pay him at times the relations between them is not strained but continued. It is not so in case of the *jajman-kamin* relations that the payments have to be, without fail, made every year.

4. In Watandari system, the services offered by the *watans* belong to the officials visiting the village. In the other two systems the services of different castes are meant for the cultivators.

5. Watadari system basically is administrative in nature whereas *jajmani* system is social and economic in nature. The dependent system basically is related to services that are social which create caste consciousness in making the main caste as the most important and superior. The services in dependent system are basically skilled arts that are meant for entertainment to the main caste and all the villagers. It may once again be noted here that the dependent castes seek alms only from the main caste and refuse to receive from other castes in the village.

6. In Watandari system, 'services' and the 'village' form as a unit. In jajmani system, services and the individual's discretion in a family become a unit.

In dependent system, services oriented toward a particular caste and the family becomes a unit in enjoying the hereditary rights.

7. In the Watandari and jajmani systems the economic considerations are primary while the social dimension is of secondary importance. In dependent system, the social relations are very important

8. In Watandari system the relations are only physical while in jajmani system they are both physical and ritualistic. In Dependent system the relations impinge on caste mythologies which spiritually reinforce the bondage between the dependent caste and the main caste.

9. Watandari system was abolished by the Government where as in case of Jajmani system the relations between *jajman* and kamin are weakened by many modern forces of change including industrialization. In dependent system also, of late, many changes are taking place, especially resulting in the diminishing patronization of the artistic skills of the dependent caste members. It was partly because of the influence of cinemas forcing many of them to leave their traditional performances. Among these three systems, Watandari system already disappeared; and the *Jajmani* system may also not survive for long but not the dependent system which is able to keep up its identity with the creation of caste myths and

caste lore. Thus the dependent system could be viewed as an independent social system. In order to understand caste myths and caste lore in the traditional relations between castes and extensions of the castes' boundaries, the study of dependent castes becomes indispensable.

The System of Dependent Relations: The system of dependent castes was formed with twin purposes. First of all, its aim is to preserve social identity by differentiating from other *gotras,* and to perpetuate their genealogies, traditions, ritual behaviour and cultural practices; the second aim is to canvass continuously that their social status is not inferior vis-à-vis other similar castes. In order to accomplish these two tasks the castes have established their own dependent castes. In order to strengthen the patron-dependent relations, the dependent castes create literature and such a literature is nothing but the caste myths, caste lore, etc. Such a literature presents: caste myths related to the origin of main caste, caste mythologies; the dependent caste's version of their caste origin or their caste mythologies which are a part and parcel of their main caste mythologies; the historical accounts of the main caste including the stories related to important individuals of their caste and their significant deeds; the periodic narration of main caste-dependent caste connections depicted in other stories. All this literature basically belonged to oral tradition, but later preserved in written accounts in case of some castes.

When caste origins were linked to mythologies, such accounts assume some kind of pious nature as divine gods and goddesses are involved. Therefore, others do not contest such origins easily. As this is mythology related it goes back to the antiquity which also brings in some honour to the caste concerned. Another most important dimension to it is that it establishes social status to the caste as one cannot evaluate one caste as superior or inferior to other caste for the simple reason that they were all created by the same divine force assigning them to perform definite tasks.

There is also a close relation between caste myths and the rituals they perform. "If we turn to living myth, that is, the myth that is believed in, we find that it has no existence apart from the ritual . . . . Knowledge of the myth is essential to the ritual because it has to be recited at the ritual" (Hocart, 1933). In village festivals different singers of different castes sing the stories of village deities.

In case of Malas and Madigas, their caste myths also present interesting findings. When their traditional cultural practices are subject to criticism and when they are required to offer some answers to questions *incomprehensible*, caste myths originate. When they are subjected to humiliation because of their caste status, naturally they try to find a way out to overcome such a humiliation. The *'Jaambava puranam'* and the related stories relate to the origins of Malas and Madigas. The origin accounts of Malas and Madigas are given in Chapter II.

In case of Malas, another caste myth is found in, *'Asaadi Maaranna',* in which the Primeval Shakti sends twelve women in her image to become the wives of *Asaadi*. Later, She declines to be the wife of *Asaadi* but when asked that she bore twelve children out of that union She replied that all of them, *'maalo vaare',* meaning that they all belong to *us* (later became *mala vaaru*). Out of these twelve women were the twelve divisions of Malas. Asaadi is a dependent caste of Malas in Rayalaseema area of Andhra Pradesh.

The Social System of Dependent Castes: It is too well known that there is traditionally a caste-occupation linkage in that every caste is assigned a traditional occupation which is still continued in case of large majority of castes in village India. In the context of such caste-occupation linkages, one such occupation is singing caste lore and reciting caste origin narratives by which some castes make a living in Andhra Pradesh for centuries. There are many historical evidences for the existence of such castes.

Those who are in the traditional occupation of singing caste lore are of two types: those who have permanent patronage and those who do not have permanent patronage. In the former case, their services of narrating caste myths and *gotras*, are rendered only to those households of the main caste with which they have traditional hereditary rights. In turn they receive alms or gifts only from them. For example the *koonapuli* caste people beg only from the saale caste. They sing songs to saale caste people—singing songs means singing their caste lore and mythological accounts of saale caste origin. When they are asked they narrate their origin stories artistically with the help of pictures. They also narrate their various *gotras* and their significance. Saale people do not invite anyone other than *koonapuli* caste for such things. For such of these services the *koonapuli* people beg for alms only the saale caste. In some cases for one main caste there are different dependent castes. For example, for the mala caste, there are in addition to *masti, gurramvaru, gotralollu, mala bhogam,* etc are the other dependent castes. Each such caste's services are considered their own and they have their own well defined rights and responsibilities which do not come into clashes with other castes. Therefore, they all become part and parcel of the same system of dependent relations.

As regards nomenclature used, those who receive these services could be differently called as 'patrons' 'jajmans', 'central caste', 'main caste', etc. Those who render these services are differently called by such names as 'dependent castes', satellite castes, 'caste beggars',*'mirasidarlu, gotralavaru, wantanagallu,* etc., which speak of their caste occupation. However, it may be noted here that these terms are used inter-changeably although the term, 'dependent castes' is used to a large extent throughout this account. The payments they receive for their services too have different names like*, wantana, mera, mirasi,* dowry, sacrifice, etc. Thus as this system is still in vogue it is found that they are called differently in different regions in Andhra Pradesh. Between the terms 'satellite castes', and 'dependent castes', the former implies more of following or imitation of the main patron castes while the later suggests total dependence on the main caste. Therefore, the preference for usage goes to 'dependent castes'.

In Andhra Pradesh[1], the *Vipravinodin,* a caste of professional conjurers to Brahmins, seeks alms only from Brahmins. Similarly the *Pitchikuntas* are bards and genealogists for the Reddy or Kapu caste. The Kammas have a wandering genealogist called *Kamma Guruvu* while *Bhatraju,* a caste of bards served the *Rajus* (Kshatriyas). Replication of such patronizing relations is found among the ex-untouchable castes who, of late, are referred to as Dalits (N.S.Reddy, 1952; T.R.Singh, 1969; Moffat, 1979; Sudhakar Rao, 2001). Reddy[2] explains that each village consists of numerically dominant castes including the Mala and Madiga having several sub-castes with a specific function in relation to the two main castes. Sudhakar Rao (2000: 94) presents the following figures depicting Caste structure in a typical village and the structure of Mala and Madiga castes.

Figure 3.1: Caste Structure in a Village

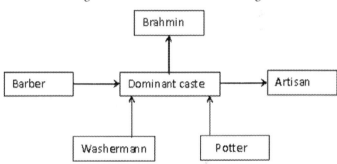

Figure 3.2: Structure of Mala and Madiga Castes

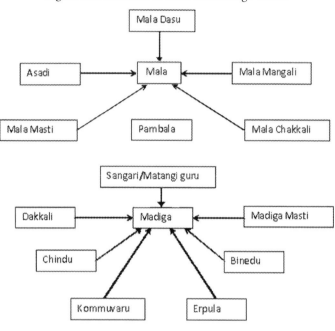

"The social structure of the untouchable caste is predicated on diverse principles such as proximity to a political and economic centre, incorporation in the village or caste system, participation in the village rituals and imitation of the political and economic power of the dominant caste. These principles underlie the most articulated idiom of the actors—purity and impurity—which until recently has been taken for granted by anthropologists" (Sudhakar Rao, 2000:95)

The *Mala Dasu* and *Matangi guru* are the priests of Mala and Madiga respectively while the *Pambala*, *Asadi*, *Erpula* and *Binedu* are the narrators of the village goddesses and ritual assistants to respective central (main) castes. *Chindollu* enact dramatic scenes from epics and

Kommuvaru are the funeral story tellers to Madiga. *Mala salikani* (weavers), *Mala mangali* (barber), *Mala chakali* (washerman), extend their specialised function to the Mala. *Dakkali* are the beggars and custodians of Madigas' legendary lore. *Beda jangam* and *Dommara* castes are also considered as satellite castes. The following is the list of dependent castes and their main castes in Andhra Pradesh. It may be noted that the list is by no means exhaustive:

TABLE 3.1: LIST OF DEPENDENT CASTES IN ANDHRA PRADESH

S.No.	DEPENDENT CASTE	MAIN CASTE
1.	VIPRA VIN0DHI	BRAHMIN
2.	VEERA MUSHTI	VAISYA, KOMATI
3.	PITCHI KUNTLA	REDDY, KAMMA
4.	KAKI PADAGALU	TELAGA, TENUGU, KAPU
5.	TENUGU BHOGAM	TELAGA, TENUGU, KAPU
6.	PANDAVULU, THOTI VAARU	MUTHRASI, MUDIRAJU
7.	TENUGU MASHTI	TELAGA, TENUGU, KAPU
8.	MANDECHULU	GOLLA, YADAVA
9.	THERA CHEERALA VAARU, GUDARU VAARU	GOLLA, YADAVA
10.	GOLLA BHAGAVATULU	GOLLA, YADAVA
11.	GOTRALA VAARU	GOLLA, YADAVA
12.	KOMMULA VAARU	GOLLA, YADAVA
13.	PEDDAMMA GUDOLLU	GOLLA, YADAVA

14.	OGGOLLU, BEERANNALA VAARU	KURUMA, KURUMA GOLLA
15.	DEVINOLLU	KURUMA, KURUMA GOLLA
16.	GOUDA JETTI, JETTOLLU	GOUNDLA
17.	YENOOTI VAALLU	GOUNDLA
18.	RUNJALU, RUNDRANGULU, RUDRA MAHESWARULU	PANCHANANAM VARU, VISHWAKARMA, VISWABRAHMANA (KAMSALI, VADRANGI, KANCHARI, KAMMARI, SHILPI)
19.	AADI PANASALU	PANCHAANANAM VARU
20.	KOMATI PANASALU	PANCHA NAAMAM VARU
21	KOONA PULI VARU, PADIGE RAJULU	SAALE, PADMA SAALE
22.	SAADHANA SOORULU	SAALE, PADMA SAALE
23.	JATI BIDDALU, JANGAALU	DEVANGULU
24.	SINGAM VARU, JANGALU	DEVANGULU
25.	AADI KODUKULU	MEDARI
26.	PATANCHKALLU, PATAM VAALLU	CHAAKALI, RAJAKA
27.	GANJIKOOTI VAARU	CHAAKALI, RAJAKA
28.	ADDHAPOLLU, ADDHAM SINGULU	MANGALI, NAAYI BRAHMANA
29.	PEKKINTI VAARU, PEKKANDRU	KUMMARI
30.	BHATTULU	REDDY, KAMMA, VELAMA
31.	BAINDLA, BAVANEELU	MADIGA

32.	PAMBHALA VAARU	MADIGA
33.	SANGADI VAARU	MADIGA
34.	AASADI	MADIGA
35.	CHINDU, CHINDU MADIGA	MADIGA
36.	MAASHTI	MADIGA
37.	DAKKALI	MADIGA
38.	GURRAM VAARU	MALA
39.	GOTRAALOLLU	MALA
40.	MALA MASTI	MALA
41.	MALA BHOGAM	MALA
42.	PAARTHANLU	GONDLU
43.	DOLUVAALLU	KOYA

Source: Caste Myths: Dependent System (in Telugu)
by P. Subbachary, Pp. 25-27

Institutionalization of Dependence Relations: The relationship between the dependent castes and the main castes is well defined and thoroughly institutionalized. The structure and function of these relationships remain and continue through generations. There are privileges as well as duties impinged on the relationship between the main castes and the dependent castes.

Binding Relationship: The traditional relationship between a caste and the attached caste(s) is one of a committed relationship. If a caste lives by the occupation of singing and telling stories, for such a performance they are paid and this relationship ends at that point by means of the payment made for such an act. But the dependent castes perform for the sake of their main caste with a sense of commitment but never the same to any other caste. The remuneration they receive is invariably from the main caste but not from any other. Here the relationship never ends

43

with receiving of some remuneration for their services. This is a permanent relationship that binds the two parties through the generations.

During the fieldwork it was noticed that the Mala Masti are in possession of copper plates on which the Royal decrees are inscribed as to the propriety of the Mala Mastis' right to collect alms from the main caste Mala and the fees prescribed for their acrobatic and muscular power shows. Thus they collect money, grain, clothes, utensils, getting cattle and other goods, even getting their marriages done by the main caste. Traditional rights sufficiently work for the Mala Masti to sustain their lives going around the villages where the main caste Malas are predominantly present. The benevolent attitude of the main caste is reinforced by the periodic praise singings they receive from the dependent caste.

The Functions of Dependent Castes: Singing of the caste lore is an important function of the Dependent castes. The Dependent caste singers have created the songs of main caste families eulogizing their genealogies. This kind of a performance is considered as invaluable by the main caste and the dependent castes as well. The caste lore is thus created in which the emergence of the genealogical line of the main caste families and their development is praised. Singing of caste lore by the satellite castes in praise of the main castes has positive effect both on the castes higher up in the hierarchy as well as lower castes. As the caste system is built on horizontal and vertical relationships in which all the castes are brought into relationships of superiority and inferiority, such a singing of caste lore tends to strengthen the superiority of upper castes while it helps to dispel the inferiority complex especially among the dalit castes.

Recitation of Geneologies and Gotras: The next most important task after the caste lore is to recite genealogical and *gotra* account. Thus some of the dependent castes have acquired the name of *'gotralavaru'*. The members of the dependent castes visiting their benevolent main caste family makes a narration of their genealogies and bless them to prosper more and more in the days to come by. For such an act they receive some payment. The Mala Mastis knowledge related to the *gotras* of the Mala caste is one main reason why their rights over the Mala families are kept intact over generations.

Caste-Occupation harmony: The dependent castes singing the caste lore also brings to light the appropriateness of their traditional occupation. The narration of their mythological origins tries to justify the traditional occupation of the main castes with a sense of pride.

Entertainment to the village folk: Some of these satellite castes also provide entertainment and amusement. For example, Mala Mastis' demonstration of different feats exhibiting their physical strength and acrobatic skills provide the much needed entertainment and amusement at the end of the day to the tired agricultural folk. The *vipravinodhins* receive alms from the Bramhins by performing magic. It may also be noted here that some of the dependent castes also provide sexual pleasures to the main caste masters.

The main (host or central) castes and their functions: Their main function is to give alms to their attached satellite caste members and providing for the daily needs of the dependent castes only. But the alms are given for the services they receive but not out of compassion or pity. For this reason, the dependent castes have acquired the names like, 'caste children', 'caste sons', 'begging children', etc. The royal decrees clearly indicate on the copper plates that they have to be treated as their own children and exhort the main caste that by giving them alms they have *'punya'*; otherwise the sin of denying would lead them to condemnation. If any one denies the alms to the dependent caste the caste council of the main caste considers it seriously and the one family which refused alms would be made outcaste. The donations made by the main castes are differently called as *dowry, begging dowry, miracy, sambhavana, vanthan, watan, ilavarasa,* sacrifice, etc.

CHAPTER IV
THE MALA MASTI

According to the 1981 census, the three Telangana districts of Karimnagar, Adilabad and Nizamabad accounted for a total of 474 Mala Mastis (people of India). The Census report implied that the Mala Mastis are present in only those three districts. The exact total population of this dependent caste is not available from any authentic source. But, this figure goes up many a time because the present study brought to light the fact that they are present in almost all the districts of Andhra Pradesh. The following table gives the total population covered in this study.

Table 4.1: Population Distribution of Mala Masti in the study villages

Name of the Village	District	Male	% of Male	Female	% of Female	Total	% of Total Population
Gollapet	Adilabad	26	5.18	31	6.70	57	3.20
Chepuru	Nizamabad	12	2.39	11	2.38	23	2.38
Gangipalli	Karimnagar	31	6.18	32	6.91	63	6.53
Nalluru	Karimnagar	19	3.78	21	4.54	40	4.15
Gorrekunta	Warangal	23	4.58	27	5.83	50	5.18
Paleru	Khammam	25	4.78	15	3.24	40	4.15
Rangapuram	Warangal	13	2.59	11	2.38	24	2.49
Beemavaram	Krishna	14	2.79	15	3.24	29	3.00
Samalkot	East Godavari	24	4.78	24	5.18	48	4.97

W.G.Gudem	East Godavari	131	26.10	108	23.33	239	24.77
Sayampalem	West Godavari	38	7.37	39	8.42	77	7.98
S.Kota	Vizianagaram	59	11.75	51	11.02	110	11.40
Chodavaram	Visakhapatnam	37	7.37	29	6.26	66	6.84
Palakonda	Srikakulam	50	9.96	49	10.58	99	10.26
Total		**502**	**100**	**463**	**100**	**965**	**100**
		52.02		**47.98**		**100**	

Mala Masti is a satellite, nomadic, dalit caste of Andhra Pradesh. They are also known as Mala *Mastin,* Mala *Masthidi,* Mala *Machachatti* and Mala *Machatollu.* They are known to make frequent visits to the Mala hamlets at regular frequency for their sustenance as eking alms is their traditional and primary occupation. They depend exclusively on the main Mala caste for alms and refuse to receive anything from other communities. During harvest times, they entertain the villagers by their songs, dances and spectacular display of acrobatics. The Mala, themselves being ex-untouchables, occupy the lowest rungs in the caste hierarchy and are mostly engaged in menial agricultural labour. We have already noted that the presence of such dependent castes is not limited to Mala caste only.

The Mala Masti Origin: According to the Mala Masti caste legend describing their origin the ancient Mala man has two wives, one married and the other the 'keep sake'. The two wives have given birth to a son each. The son born to the married wife is making a living by hard work. The other one was begging from all others. In the antiquity, at the place where they were living, seven Kings who were brothers were ruling the land. Each one of them was courageous, strong and powerful and all of them were experts in war skills like fighting with swords and sticks. Among them the youngest one is an expert in acrobatics and a long poll used to be his aid on which he used to climb up and practice. The 'beggar' son of the Mala used to watch the King's varied skills and himself started learning those things without the knowledge of the King but just by observing from a distance. While things were going like that the 'goldsmith' *(Kamsali)* caste has a *Kamsali* Masti who was very courageous, powerful and knew magical powers. He used to eat a goat a day and one or two hen every day. If he sits he used to look like the trunk of a *chinta* (tamarind) tree and when he stands he looked like, *thaati* (Palm) tree that grows very tall. He used to move around all the villages and seduced all the women he liked. He imposed his will on all the villagers and accordingly if there was a girl present in any family he conditioned that the parents of the girl themselves should send her to him voluntarily. Malas too fell in line with all others helplessly with such a condition. Thus, every one feared this Kamsali Masti and if any one refuses to send their daughters he used to beat them to death. It was his pastime to tease the womenfolk who go to the village tank to fetch water. Every married women he assumed was first his wife only by proclaiming that he was a bridegroom for ever for all. He reasoned that the husbands tie the *thali* (the bridegroom ties this around the neck of the bride during marriage ceremony as a symbol of marriage) only once but the *thalis* (made of gold) are made by him (as the Kamsalis only make them) for all so that he was actually their husband first. As this was going on like that, the wife of the Chief of Malas made all the women assemble and declared that it was no good with their husbands and it did not matter whether their husbands were alive or dead as they were unable to protect their honour. Eventually they revolted against their husbands and when the Mala Chief asked his wife to serve him food she dug a small pit in the corner of the house in which she kept some cooked food together with her *thali*. Surprised by this strange act the Chief asked her why she was doing like that for which she replied that when the Kamsali Masti declared himself as the husband for all the women there was no need for her to have a husband like him and even if he were alive he was as good as dead. Infuriated by these utterances he came out of the home only to find out that every Mala had the same experience with their wives. Then all the Malas with their Chief assembled and seriously thought over the solution to their problem.

Next morning they initiated a search for someone who can defeat the *Kamsali* Masti. They accosted the one beggar son of the 'keep sake' wife who heard the whole episode as they narrated him of their insults at the hands of their wives. After listening to their plight he asked them to seek audience with the King and ask for a fight between the Kamsali Masti and Malas and in the interim he would keep the cattle in the shed. When the Mala chief expressed that there was no competent fighter among them to take on the Kamasali Masti the 'beggar boy' replied that he himself would defeat him. All those assembled got surprised listening to that boy. As there was no other way they went to the King who assented for such a fight.

Accordingly, the Kamsali Masti and the Mala boy entered the ring for a fight. Both were given a sword and a shield each. The only condition of the fight was that in three attempts one should kill the other. The first three attempts were offered to the Kamsali Masti voluntarily by the Mala boy. On listening to this offer the Kamsali Masti laughed at him saying 'why do you invite death by fighting me. As you are a kid ask for my mercy I will let you go'. But the boy refused saying 'if I am going to die I would not have come this far. I am ready for the fight'. Then they both got ready for a fight. All the three times the boy escaped from the hands of the Kamsali Masti. At the time when the boy wielded his sword, the Kamsali Masti as he has magical powers, got suddenly disappeared and assumed the shape of a banana tree carrying a bunch of bananas. The Mala boy's mother informed his son that the Kamsali Masti was in the form of the banana tree which was his body and the bunch of bananas were nothing but his hands. After listening to his mother he caught hold of the bunch and cut it off from the trunk. Immediately the Kamsali Masti made his presence with a sword running through his right hand and left hands. Kamsali Masti wisely, without lifting his hands, sneered at the boy saying that 'You cannot do anything to me' for which the boy replied that 'he had stabbed him using only one attempt that leaves him with two more chances and he was not going to use his sword any more to kill him'. The mother asked the boy to do *namaskarams* (salutations) to the King and others by lifting his hands which he did and asked the Kamsali Masti to do the same. But when the Kamsali Masti did not agree for that the King commanded him to do the *namaskarams* lifting his hands. As he lifted his hands air entered the wounds of his body and caused heavy bleeding. As a result he instantly died. The King and the people present were astonished by the courageous act of the boy and the King granted the boy whatever he wished even if that included the villages, gold or money. But the boy replied that he did not want villages, gold or money and that he was born to his father's 'keep sake'. 'Every caste had a Masti but to Mala caste there was no Masti.

between them. The husband looks after the pregnant wife with every possible care by helping her in all the tasks she usually performs.

Plate 1: A Part of the Raagi Patta—Copper plate inscription

Social Organization: Their social organization is based on the surname groupings. The following table 4.2 gives a list of surnames of the Mala Masti in the villages studied:

**Table 4.2: Showing a village-wise list
of surnames of Mala Masti**

Sl. No	Surname	Name of the Village	District
1	Nulaka	Singannavalasa	Srikakulam
2	Malisetti		
3	Devupalli		
4	Nethala		
5	Doosi		
6	Jangam		
7	Kandipalli	Srungavarapukota	Vizianagaram
8	Nulaka		
9	Malisetti		
10	Chikala	Chodavaram	Visakhapatnam
11	Nulaka		
12	Malisetti		
13	Sikala		
14	Kandipalli		
15	Vadde	Vechalam	
16	Kaki	West Gonagudem	East Godavari
17	Pathi		
18	Talluru		
19	Malisetti		
20	Vadde	Velanka	
21	Sikala	Bandanapudi	
22	Nulaka	Samalkot	
23	Malisetti		
24	Yedla		
25	Talluru		
26	Pulagaru	Sayampalem	West Godavari
27	Tydula		
28	Medi		
29	Bitra		
30	Bitra		
31	Uddagiri		

32	Pulagaru	Paleru	Khammam
33	Tydula		
34	Mara	Gorrekunta	Warangal
35	Dyagala		
36	Resu	Rangapuram	
37	Mara	Gangipalli	Karimnagar
38	Dyagala		
39	Bitla	Chepuru	Nizamabad
40	Dyagala		
41	Bitla	Nalluru	
42	Dyagala		
43	Vijjagiri		
44	Bitla	Gollapet (Nirmal)	Adilabad
45	Dyagala		
46	Vijjagiri		

Gotras among the Mala Masti: *Gotra* is an equivalent of clan in the Indian context. Surnames refer to patrilineal descent with the exception of very few matrilineal societies in India, and the women folk take the surname of fathers till they get married and after marriage they take the surname of their husbands. Those who have the surname, 'nulaka' belong to the 'Naga (snake)' gotra and they do not celebrate Nagula chaviti (snake festival) and Deepavali (festival of lights) for a belief that these festivals do not bring any good to them. If they celebrate they may come across any type of bad event in their lives. This is traditionally believed among them. Those who have '*malisetty*' surname belong to the '*matsya* (fish) gotra' and do not kill any fish. They go for fishing but the fish are killed by others. Mala Masti of North Coastal Andhra region perform '*trimoorty pooja*' and worship the god '*simhadri appanna*'. In Telangana Area, all the Mala Mastis belong to only one gotra by name' *recharla gotra*'.

Kinship terms: Kinship relations are very strong among the Mala Masti. All the relatives are given a lot of respect. The Father is addressed as *'appa'* but of late, like others around them adopted the more sanskritised term *'naanna'*. The father's relatives are considered as the primary relatives and the Mother's relatives are considered as of secondary importance with the only exception of the maternal uncle who is very much revered and is given a place equivalent to one's father by addressing him as *'naanna'*. Now they are addressing him as *'maamayya* (uncle) under the influence of others around them.

Life Cycle Ceremonies: Pregnancy is an important stage of *rites de passage*. After marriage once menstruation is stopped pregnancy is determined. In the 5th month or 7th month the pregnant woman is taken home by her parents. It may be noted here that many of the Mala Masti families have now settled residences in many villages. Till the delivery is over she is looked after well by her parents. Now and then the husband visits her. Once the labour pains start the mother immediately informs of it to the neighbours. Then the mid-wife known to them also is informed. The mid-wife may belong to Mala caste or any other caste. Then the delivery is conducted and in critical cases the pregnant woman is advised to go to the hospital. If a male child is delivered the woman's father and the father of the child in their respective villages make a loud village announcement. The caste leaders are paid 6 rupees by the child's father. Since then the allotment of a share in the villages roamed around by this family to this new born child is made. This child is given 25% of all the collections once he is grown up till his marriage. Once his marriage is fixed he gets 50% of the collections. After the marriage he gets a full 100% of the share. If the female child is delivered the child gets whatever the expenses she has to maintain herself. She gets a measure of rice and one rupee and the male child gets double the measure of the grain. If it is a female child the caste leaders are paid three rupees. The child is given a bath with luke-warm water immediately after the delivery. The umbilical cord is cut by the midwife with a small knife. These days she is using a new blade every time. After bath the child is fed with mother's milk. To remove the waste material from the mother's womb, *inguva* (asafoetida) with black *jaggery* (black sugar) is cooked in oil and this is fed to the mother of the child. If the milk of the mother is insufficient, some local ingredients are made into a paste and the child is fed with it. After delivery the mother is fed only once a day. Every day at 10 in the morning food is given to her. Coriander seeds, *jeera* (cumin seeds) and *vaamu* (tymol seeds) are ground together and she is fed this with oil. Old rice is cooked and the mother is fed. In *Malapalli,* (the hamlet where the Malas reside) if some household cooks the old rice she collects it to eat. It is believed that eating like this makes the mother's body strong by removing all unwanted water and the child also would be healthy. The mother is given a bath on the third day while the child is given bath every day. The ceremonial bath is given on the 9th day by applying turmeric powder all over the mother's body and the relatives are given a feast. After the bath the mother wears a new sari given by her in-laws. Along with the sari, a bath soap and *gingelli* (sesame) oil are given to her. In the afternoon the men drink liquor with some special dish (*nalla koora*). After the feast every one disperses to their respective homes.

Name Giving Ceremony: The child is given a name within a year of its birth. Usually in the 6th month the child is ceremonially given first feeding and on that day the child is given a name. The names given are usually of the ancestors of the father. The near relatives numbering around 10 are invited on this occasion and they are given food on this day. But in Maddur Lanka village it was informed that naming the child is done in the 3rd month or 6th month and the child is called by any name they like. There is no observance of ceremonial first feeding of the child. The child is usually given foods which are easily digested.

Tonsure Ceremony: The first removal of the child's hair is done ceremonially within the first year. The child is given a bath in the morning on that day and if there is any vow made by the parents, the hair is removed only at such of those places of pilgrimage, otherwise it is done at home. In Maddur Lanka village on the day the child's hair is removed the child's mother's brother (maternal uncle) is invited who removes initially hair at three places on the head and the remaining job is done by the barber. The males can have their hair removed any number of times before marriage. After marriage such a clean shave is not permitted, because they have to use their hair to pull heavy objects on a show.

Ear Piercing: The female child has to undergo this ritual. When her ear is to be pierced, if the maternal grandparents are rich enough they buy gold ear rings for the girl. If the grand parents aren't that rich the parents of the girl buy the rings. This is done in the first year of the child at the goldsmith's place.

Adoption: The childless couples in the good old days have to remain forever without children. Now-a—days the children are adopted from the families of the close relatives without any formal agreements or registration. This is done by the consent of the caste elders.

Puberty: After the girl comes of age she informs the mother first who in turn informs all those women around her. Immediately the maternal uncle of the child is informed who immediately attends and the child is made to sit on a mat made of palm leaves. The women around their home attend with small quantities of rice and sprinkle it around the girl and a banana with a cocoanut are placed on the rice. Every day only dal with rice is served her but not any curry. On the ninth day a ceremonial bath is given her. On that day the mat on which the girl sat all these days is thrown outside the boundaries of the village as it is considered polluted and a potential carrier of evil. On the 9th day near relatives numbering about 50 are invited to share the food and the maternal uncle brings new clothes to the girl. All of them bless the girl sprinkling rice mixed with turmeric powder on the head of the girl. The men enjoy liquor on that occasion and by evening all of them depart to their respective places.

Marriage: Marriages are usually arranged by the elders. The cross cousin marriages are much preferred among them. If the suitable cross cousins are not available those who stand in the same relationship are preferred. If a suitable girl is available the parents of the boy approach them with a proposal. If the girl's parents agree to the proposal they ask them to bring the elders. If they are not willing they tell them that they are not in a hurry to get their daughter married just to avoid such a proposal. If they are willing, the elders decide on an auspicious date and the girl's parents are informed to 'spread the mat' on that day. On that day the girl's parents ask their elders to attend and the boy's parents bring a mat with them for their elders to sit on the mat in the girl's house. After that the elders from both the sides sit together with two tumblers full of water in front of them. Then on behalf of the boy 6 rupees and on behalf of the girl 3 rupees are placed before them. Then the bride-price is negotiated which may go up to a maximum of 1000 rupees. If the negotiations are agreed to both sides the water in the two tumblers is mixed and they drink it together. This ceremony is called *'kalagallu'*. The elders take the mixed water first followed by the parents and others of both sides.

Since then the girl is referred to as daughter-in-law of 'so and so'. The Brahmin fixes the auspicious day for betrothal. In the good old days the elders themselves used to fix the auspicious day. The bride-to-be is made to wear a *'bondhu'* which is made of five strands of thick thread smeared with turmeric and blessed by the married women.

The marriage is performed at the boy's house. When the boy has sufficient money then only the marriage is performed. The money needed for the marriage is provided by the elders (from Mala caste) of the villages where they move around. In one such village only the marriage is performed. On the day of marriage in front of the boy's house a *neredu* (Mytus cyminum) tree branch or mango or *maredu* (the Bael of Bel fruit tree) is placed. After that a *pandal* made of palm leaves, is erected with 12 columns. On the first day the boy's party carries the requirements of the marriage together with the presents to the bride that include a *saree,* sweets and fruits and they go to the girl's place where they are fed. After the lunch, they return to the groom's place with the bride. On that day the bride's party is lodged in a separate house. For that night food is arranged to all of them by the groom's party.

On the next day the girl is taken around the village in a procession. In the evening the bride and the groom are made to sit in the *pandal* (a temporary structure (shed) erected for the marriage) and given a ceremonial bath with turmeric with five pots of tank water. The *'Bajigallu'* (drum-beaters) who are from Mala caste make the groom to tie the *'thali'.* Now-a-days the Brahmin priest is performing this task in some places as some of them now lead settled lives as in case of Korukonda. The Maternal uncle presents toe-rings to the bride. The presents from both sides which are called *'eedethalu'* are announced. On the third day *'aviredu'* ceremony is performed in which a ring and other things made of gold, silver or copper is kept within a pot full of water. The bride and the groom are then asked to find it. Whoever finds the most valuable item is playfully considered greater. Then procession is taken around the village with groom wearing a head gear and *panche* (a traditional cloth covering from the waist to the feet) on the horse back with the bride following it on the ground. The marital status of Mala Masti in study villages is given in Annexure-I.

Divorce: Divorce is allowed when the married couple so decide with the consent of the elders. The elders try their best to reconcile unless there are grave charges like infidelity. They can re-marry after divorce. If they have children they stay with the father but in some cases the female children stay with their mother. When the children stay with their mother, the mother usually do not get re-married.

Death: The dead are buried in the same burial ground meant for the Malas. Death may occur due to ill health and also due to black magic. After death dried up fodder is spread on the ground over which a *panche* or a saree is placed. The corpse is placed on it. A pesticide to ward off the ants is sprinkled around the body. A small lamp is placed at the head with incense lighting up. After the arrival of the relatives four of them with two bottles of liquor are sent to the burial ground to dig a pit. After their return the corpse is smeared with turmeric and it is given a bath. A washed *panche* or *saree,* depending on the sex of the deceased, is used to carry the corpse on the hands to the burial ground. But at present the corpse is carried on a pyre made of wooden sticks. When it is carried to the burial ground the followers sing songs to the beating of the drums. The head is placed toward south and the legs toward north while burying the corpse. In their return all of them take a bath in a tank nearby. By the time they return a lamp is lighted at the house. In front of the house in a small container a small quantity of cow dung is placed and all of them are supposed to step over it seeing the lamp and then only they enter the home. This is done with a belief of warding off the evil associated with the dead corpse.

On the third day three of the relatives go to the tomb and tie up 'thirupalu' which is burying a stone at the foot and another at the head. On the third day which is called 'chinna dinam', food is served to all the relatives. After the food is cooked they carry the 'padi' (chicken, fish, bird's meat, brinjal (eggplant) curry and other items, together with three pan cakes, and sweets made of jaggery) to the tomb. If the death is that of a woman, the husband or the father or the brothers perform the rituals. In case of men, the eldest son or the father performs the rituals. One bottle of liquor is carried to the burial ground which is called 'varakam'. The liquor is sprinkled in three directions and the remaining liquor is drunk by the elders. A cocoanut is broken after burning some incense and lighting a lamp at the tomb. Those who perform the rituals distribute the food to all those who attend the rituals after offering some part of it to the tomb. Then at the foot side and at the head side stones are buried. This is made to make known that this tomb is that of Mala Masti. On the third day if the family of the dead fails to provide liquor to others they agree to do so on the eleventh day ceremony which is the 'pedda dinam'.

On the eleventh day about 50 or 70 of the relatives gather at the house of the deceased. A pig is slaughtered for the occasion and cooked. Rice, brinjal (eggplant) curry, dal, rasam and 200 ariselu (local sweet) are made and small quantities of them are thrown into the village canal. When a canal is not present these are mixed in a vessel. After that all of them eat the food and depart. On the thirteenth day they move on to another village. The Malas cooperate with the Mala Masti on such occasions in giving fire wood and also cash but they do not dine with them.

However in West Gonagudem village as the pollution lasts for 21 days those who perform the ritual are not supposed to leave the village. Therefore, one day less than a months' time is appropriate for them to leave the village.

In Military Madahavaram village in West Godavari district, the *pedda dinam* is performed on the 7th day. On that day the widow's bangles are broken and the *bottu* (a dot sported on the forehead of Hindu women and girls) is removed and she is made to wear a white *saree* (a symbol of widowhood). From that day onward one can see her face. In Paleru of Khammam district, either the one son who performed the ritual or the widower's head is clean shaved. The widower is not supposed to wear the waist string. If he gets married again he can wear it afterwards. In Gangipalli village of Karimnagar district the tomb is plastered with cement on the 5th day. On the 11th day afternoon all the caste people contribute together 30 to 50 rupees and have food at the burial ground. They also feed free to those who belong to the household of the dead. In the evening they in turn arrange food for all of them. After consuming the food in the evening all of them sing songs, caste lore and other narratives. The relatives bring clothes to the household members of the deceased. In the morning all of them depart to their respective villages. The Mala *dasari* performs the ritual on the 11th day at the burial ground.

Tattooing: As the Mala Mastis throw very heavy objects in to the air and take the falling objects on to their shoulders and arms in a bid to publicly exhibit their physical strength, they usually suffer from body pains. Tattooing is done to the bodily parts that are prone to suffer from pain with a belief that the pains would recede by such tattooing. Sometimes names and pictures are tattooed fancifully on their arms. The Mala Masti women used to do this tattooing earlier by moving around the neighboring villages. They used to do tattooing for other castes also. By this they used to earn about Rs.50/—a day. It is customary that the tattooing women should return home immediately after the job is over without staying anywhere, no matter what the time is. Otherwise, they are subjected to pay a fine to the caste *sangham* (council) and also get beaten up by their husband/father.

Nomadic Movement: Still a large number of them are found to be nomadic although a good number of them have settled themselves in villages with their own houses. As they are traditionally nomadic, they move in groups. As they do not carry much luggage, a horse is used to carry their belongings. A few of them carry their belongings themselves. When the path-ways are difficult to tread on they used to slaughter a pig as a sacrifice. Otherwise, it is believed that they would encounter a danger. It may be noted that the data for this study were mostly collected from settled Mala Masti in the study villages. They move around villages within a radius of 20 to 30 kilometers, where Malas are present in good numbers and from whom to collect alms.

Musical instruments: The implements and instruments needed for their trade are made by themselves. The things they need for their show, '*paata (aata).* such as, *sitara* (one stringed musical instrument), *jamuku* (percussion instrument), *dakki* (drum), *nagara* (big drum made of cow's skin) are made by themselves. They hunt for small birds and crows with a small implement called

65

'intillabadda'. For fishing they use a fishing rod with a hook. The women make mats with *palmyra* trees leaves.

Daily Activities: Children below the age of 5 years stay with the mother. After the 5th year the sons move with the father and the children stay with the mother. Between the ages 6 to 15 the girls attend the household work including fetching water and helping the mother in cooking etc, The boys help in getting fodder to the goats. They also accompany the father in going out for fishing. They learn the arts connected with acrobatic feats and weighing heavy materials. Of late, in settled villages the children are found attending the schools.

The girls get married during the age of 15 and 18. Earlier they used to get married by 12 years of age. In case of boys the age at marriage earlier used to be between 16 and 18 but now-a—days it has gone up to 20 to 25. If the boys learn the skills of *'fireman'* (the skills of weighing heavy objects and throwing them into the air etc.) the boys get married only after 25 years of age. After marriage from 3 to 6 months they stay with their parents. After that they are allocated some villages by the father and in such of those villages they have rights to beg and stay. But many of them are now eking out their lives as menial labourers, working as coolies. The women collect alms and are expected to perform house-keeping. But at present, many of them also work as coolies. The men beat the drums at 4.30 in the morning. After eating food at 9 a.m. in the morning they take out the goats for grazing. There, if possible, they do a little bit of fishing and again at 6 p.m. they beat the drums. After eating food in the night they indulge in learning skills associated with their traditional exhibition of physical strength. All those over and above 50 years are left to mend themselves as the children establish their own families. Those who earlier worked as firemen carry out their own activities of daily living because of their physical fitness. Then women confine themselves to home with occasional collection of alms.

Economic Status: Their average annual income is reported to be in the range of Rupees 15,000-20,000. From each and every household of the Malas in the Malapalli hamlet, an amount of Rupees Ten is collected by the Mala Headman and it is meant for the 'other' expenses of these Mala Masti. If they perform in the village in addition to the ten rupees another contribution of forty to fifty rupees is paid them. This money is collected over a period of three to five months to be paid to the Mala Mastis on the day of performance. If someone in the crowd, impressed by the feats performed by any artiste, announces an additional gift of 100 rupees that amount goes to that particular artiste only. In addition to this kind of income they also generate some more income by goats rearing and tending them. Goats are taken along with them wherever they go. Occasional fishing also supplements their income. The money thus earned is spent on their marriages, liquor, clothing and other expenses. The one who lives in a village invites Mala Masti in other villages to join him on the day of performance so that the collected money is shared among them with the lions share going to the one who invited them. This kind of a mutual cooperation sustains them as a group. With more and more Mala Mastis opting for settled life, there is a growing tendency among them for occupational mobility. Their children started attending the schools and a few them are found going to the colleges.

The occupational distribution of the Mala Masti in the study villages is given in the Annexure – II.

From the tables one can easily notice that majority of them are engaged as construction labourers. In case of Srikakulam district firewood is collected from the forest and it is sold in the nearby market. In S.Kota many of them are working in the quarry in breaking big boulders. They are all manual labourers.

Political Status: All the same surname families constitute a lineage and each lineage got a head man, assisted by two members and a *saladu* (messenger). They are elected in annual meetings of the lineage *(sangham)*. Those who are elderly, acceptable and knowledgeable are generally elected to these positions. This annual meeting of the lineage (*sangham*) is usually convened in the month of March every year. All the money matters settled in the last meeting with dues have to be paid in this meeting. From this amount a small portion of it is spent toward liquor and the remaining amount is kept with the leaders. The Caste association meeting (federation of caste *sanghams*) is convened once in every three years and the members are one from each *sangham*. This money is deposited to the caste association. In case arbitration of the last *sangham* meeting is not agreeable to the members it is presented before the caste association (federation). Till the dispute is settled, irrespective of the time taken for such a purpose, the members of the caste association do not leave the place where the meeting is convened. The following tables give information related to the members of the caste associations in Amalapuram area of East Godavari district:

**Table 4.3: Showing Surname level
Political Organization in Amalapuram* area**

Sl. No.	Name	Position
1	Talluru Nagaraju	*Peda Masti*
2	Talluru Nallasubbaiah	President
3	Talluru Yesu	Vice President
4	Talluru Ravi	Member
5	Talluru Venkanna	*Saladu/ Bantrothu*

- *In East Godavari; Peda Masti is an elderly man; Saladu is the Messenger*

**Table 4.4: Showing Caste level
Political Organization in East Godavari District**

Sl. No.	Name	Position
1	Pathi Peda Subbarao	*Peda Masti*
2	Pathi Annavaram	President
3	Talluru Jagapathi Rao	Vice President
4	Talluru Ramudu	Member
5	Talluru Moshaiah	Member
6	Pathi Krishna Murthy	Member
7	Talluru Nagaraju	Member
8	Sikala Chiranjeevi	Member
9	Talluru Venkateswarlu	Member
10	Pathi Nageswara Rao	Member
11	Sikila Bheemudu	Saladu/ Bantrothu

Educational Status: Their educational status is very low as in case of a nomadic group. Most of them are illiterate and a few of them have just reached intermediate as they started sending their children very recently. Gaining benefits of education is possible only in case of the settled villages like Korukonda and Singannavalasa where children are sent to school since 10-15 years. The Mala Masti educational status in the study villages is given in Annexure—III. It may be observed that the girl child education suffers at all levels in all the villages in comparison to boys' education.

Religion: They are Hindus by religion and they worship a deity named *'Bethala'*. He is none other than *'Anjaneya'*, the monkey god, who is associated with *Lord Rama,* the Hindu high God. They also worship *Bethala's* sister, *Durgalamma.* Once in a year they act in a play in which one of them plays the female role of *Durgalamma.* On the next day they worship *Anjaneya* because he is considered as mighty god so that they also can perform mighty deeds. On the day of *Dasara* Festival which falls in the month of October, a pig is sacrificed to *Anjaneya* and *Durgalamma* and the blood is smeared to their instruments like knifes, daggers, shields, drums etc. they break a coconut and worship these two deities by burning incense. On *Sivarathri* day, which usually falls in the month of February, they worship '*Simhadri Appanna*' a local god in Visakhapatnam. But now-a-days they are worshipping all the Hindu gods and goddesses. A few of them are also converting themselves into Christianity.

Their belief system: They believe in the existence of supernatural beings including devils and demons. When a person is possessed by any evil spirit the neighbors call for the services of the magicians to drive away the evil spirit. The Magician comes to know who possessed the person and draws a certain design on the ground and makes the person sit in it and utters magical spells to ward off the evil spirits. For every visit the magician is paid an amount of Rs.100-200.

When they come across any bad omen they invariably sacrifice a pig. Even on occasions like marriages, changing their residences, caste meetings and other festivals including the life cycle ceremonies, they sacrifice a pig. When any of their belongings accidentally drop down to earth from the horse back, while on a ride, they consider it as a bad omen. Some parts of the sacrificed pig, like the mouth, ears, fat on the neck and the tail are cooked separately without cutting them into pieces. When they have liquor then each piece is broken into smaller ones and eaten. The family with the surname *'malisetti'* takes first the mouth parts as they are the oldest inhabitants. Later, *'the nulaka'* surname family has the right to pick up the parts of the ear and then the *sikila* and *chikala* families take the neck fat. At the end stand the *kandipalli* family who consume the tail part. They contribute to their caste association by paying some cash to retain this privilege of rights exclusively over the respective parts of the pig. For example, the *malisetti* family pays rupees 30 for the mouth parts; the *nulaka* family 20 rupees for the ears; *sikala* family divides the neck fat into two parts: *jamula silalu* and *vidi silalu*. The *jamula silalu* are three in number and for which they pay rupees five each and for *vidi silalu* they pay 6 rupees each by the *chikala* family. *Kandipalli* family pays rupees nine to the tail part. With this money they buy liquor together and consume their respective parts of the pig.

Relations between Mala and Masti: All economic relations make the Masti to depend solely on the Malas. The Masti consider themselves as inferior to Malas and the Malas also maintain it. Any function celebrated by Mastis is attended invariably by the Malas but the Malas do not partake in the feast hosted by the Mastis except accepting liquor. The raw meat is accepted but not the cooked dishes. For such occasions the Malas give them rice, tamarind, red-chilly powder over and above what they usually give them. The Mala elders and their women are respected by the Mastis. Others are called by fictitious kin terms.

Recent Changes: Things have changed a little recently. The Masti usually roam around the villages totally depending on the Malas. But now-a—days, they are settling in villages where they have good name and contacts as in the case of West Gonegudem. They made a permanent settlement in this village 15 years ago. They are working as coolies and their children are getting educated in schools. In some cases there are inter-caste marriages too. Some of them are converting themselves to Christianity under the influence of the main Mala caste. As the Malas got converted to Christianity they stopped the age old practice of giving alms to these Masti.

There are strained relations in some places between the Malas and Mala Masti especially due to instances of love marriages between these communities which are basically endogamous. In Singannavalasa of Srikakulam district separate places are demarcated for the Malas and Mala Mastins in using the village tank. On one day the youth of both these castes came into clashes when the Mala youth tried to insult the Masti and the Masti youth retaliated and fought with each other. A police case was registered. After some time a Masti boy eloped with a Mala girl which caused the Mala caste to take a hostile attitude toward the entire Mala Masti caste. The Masti boy maintains that the Mala girl got attracted toward him because of the skills he exhibited during the shows (aata). Such strained relations are being continued till today.

In another similar case in Palakonda, a Masti boy and a Telaga caste girl got married without the consent of the elders. The girl was beaten up and taken away by the Telaga caste people. But the girl reached him back and got admitted into the Masti caste as the boy paid a *'thappu'*(a penalty imposed by the caste council) of Rupees two thousand. The girl was declared out-caste by the girl's parents one year ago.

The routes the Mala Masti take in visiting their patron Malas of other nearby villages:

The Mala Mastis periodically visit, along with their family members, their main caste Malas living in other villages, other than their own settled village, taking almost regular routes to collect their alms. The following two cases, taken from West Gonegudem (Naidu, 2011) settled Mala Masti, amply illustrate the routes the Mala Masti family takes every year and the distances of each and every village, and the length of their stay in each village in such visits are given. The amounts that are collected during such visits by each and every family are given. It may be noted that during such visits the entire Mala Masti family stays on the verandahs of their benevolent Mala hosts rotating among them.

Case Study 1 of a Settled Mala Masti Family in West Gonegudem: The routes they take in visiting the Main caste Malas (patrons) in other villages

Diagram – 1

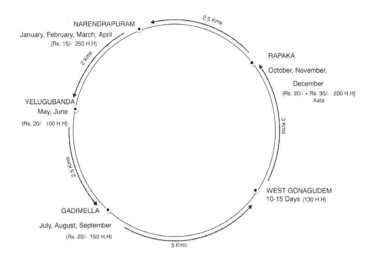

Sl.No	Name of the Village	Amount	Name of the Family Members
1	Rapaka	10,000-00	Kaki Yesu Babu-Head (30)
2	Narendrapuram	3,750-00	Kaki Seshamma-Wife (27)
3	Yelugubanda	2,000-00	Kaki Kumari-Daughter (8)
4	Gadimella	3,000-00	Kaki Johnbabu—Son (6)
	Total	18,750-00	Kaki Joseph-Son (3)
	Aata expenses (deducted)	5,000-00	
	Annual Net Income	13,750-00	

Kaki Yesubabu lives in the village West Gonegudem with his family members. He owns a house in this village but stays hardly for about a fortnight and the rest of the time in the year moves around in the villages where he has his patrons from the main Mala Caste. The route he usually takes in visiting these villages and the distance from West Gonegudem and the length of stay in those villages, are shown in the diagram number 1. The money he usually collects in those villages is shown in the table given below the diagram.

From the diagram it can be seen that Yesubabu with his family visits Rapaka village, 3 kilometers (kms) from west Gonegudem, which has 200 House Holds (HH), and stays there from October to November, every year. There his collection amounts to Rupees (Rs). 10,000/-. From there he goes to Narendrapuram, 2.5 kms from Rapaka, which has 250 HH of Malas and the amount collected from each Mala HH is Rs.15/-. Thus an amount of 3,750 is collected from this village. He stays there from January to April.

From there he moves to Yelugubanda, 2 kms from Narendrapuram, which has 100 HH of Malas from whom he collects Rs.20 per HH. Thus an amount of Rs.2000/—is collected. He stays there for two months, May and June.

From there he goes to Gadimella, 2.5 kms from Yelugubanda, with 150 HHs and the collection from each HH is Rs.20. Thus an amount of Rs.3000/ is collected there. He stays there for three months from July to September.

Finally, he comes back to West Gonegudem which is 3 kms from Gadimella, during the last week of September or First week of October. This is approximately the usual annual movements of Yesu Babu's family. His net income is 13,750/—after deducting Rs.5000/—toward 'aata' expenses.

Case Study 2 of a Settled Mala Masti Family in west gonegudem: The routes they take in visiting the Main caste Malas (patrons) in other villages

Diagram—2

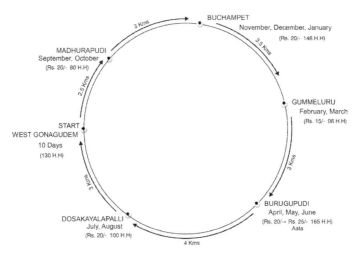

Sl.No	Name of the Village	Amount	Name of the Family Members
1	Madhurapudi	1,600-00	Kaki Veeraswami
2	Buchampet	2,920-00	Rao-Head (28)
3	Gummeluru	1,470-00	Kaki Venkatalaxmi-Wife (24)
4	Burugupudi	7,425-00	Kaki Nirmala-Daughter (8)
5	Dosakayalapalli	2,000-00	Kaki Chiranjeevi-Son (6) Kaki Nagendra-Son (5)
Total		15,415-00	
Aata expenditure (deducted)		4,200-00	
Annual Net Income		11,215-00	

The above diagram 2, shows the routes Kaki Venkata Rao and his family takes in visiting the Main Mala Patrons in other villages. He visits Madhurapudi, 2.5 kms from

West Gonegudem, with a total 80 HH of Malas, from September to October every year. With each Mala HH contributing Rs.20/-, he collects Rs.1600/—from that village.

From there he moves to Buchampeta, 3 kms away from Madhurapudi, which has 146 Mala HH who contribute Rs.20 per HH. Thus he collects Rs. 2920/ from that village during his stay from November to January. From there travelling 3.5 kms by foot, as always, he reaches Gummeluru, which has 98 HH of Malas who contribute Rs.15/—per HH during his stay from February to March.

From there he goes to Burugupadu, travelling 3 kms which has165 HH of Malas who contribute Rs 20/—and an addition of Rs.25/ toward 'aata'. Thus an amount of Rs 7,425/ is usually collected from this village during his stay from April to June every year. From there he moves to Dosakayalapalli, 4 kms from Burugupady, which has 100 Mala HHs who contribute Rs.20 per HH. Thus an amount of Rs.2000/—is collected from this village during his stay from July to August.Finally, from there he returns to West Gonegudem during the last week of August or First week of September. His total net income per annum is Rs 11,215/—after deducting Rs.4200 toward 'aata' expenses.

Nomadism and dependence: The nomadic Mala Masti keep moving from village to village seeking alms from their patron Malas in villages assigned to them hereditarily. In some of those villages they perform *'aata'* for which they collect more than they usually get from the Mala Households. The interesting aspect is that an average Masti family earns an amount of Rs. 15,000—20,000 like this. This is comparable to the amount that is earned by the Masti of a settled village like the West Gonegudem.

For this reason, still a few Mala Masti families in West Gonegudem go around villages and collect alms although they can as well work as agricultural coolies and earn their living. Two cases of the nomadic Mala Masti families who do not own any house anywhere are given here under.

Case Study 1 of a Mala Masti Nomadic Family:
The routes they take in visiting the Main caste
Malas (patrons) in other villages
Diagram 3

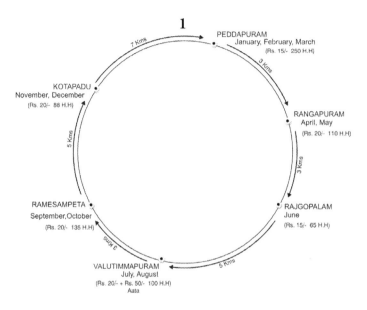

Sl.No	Name of the Village	Ammount	Name of the Family Members
1	Pedddapuram	3,750-00	Pathi Venkateswara
2	Rangapuram	2,200-00	Rao-Head (29)
3	Rajagopalam	975-00	Pathi Ganga-Wife (24)
4	Valuthimmapuram	7,000-00	Pathi Kanakamahalaxmi-
5	Ramesampeta	2,700-00	Daughter (5)
6	Kotapadu	1,760-00	
	Total	18,385-00	
	Aata expenditure (deducted)	4,000-00	
	Annual Net Income	14,385-00	

Pathi Venkateswara Rao doesn't own a house anywhere. He just moves from one village to the other, where his patron Malas live, with his family consisting of his wife and daughter. From the Diagram-3, it can be seen that from Peddapuram, where he stayed from January to March collecting Rs.3750/—from 250Mala HH at the rate of (@) Rs.50 per HH, he moves to Rangapuram village, 3 kms away which has 110 Mala HH. He collects Rs.20 per HH there after staying there for two months in April and May.

From there he moves to Rajgopalam, 3 kms from Rangapuram, which has 65 Mala HHs and he collects Rs. 975 there @Rs.15/—per HH during his stay in the month of June. From there he travels 5 kms to reach Valuthimmapuram where he collects Rs.7000/—from the 100 Mala HHs @2o per HH and @50 per HH toward 'aata' during his stay in July and August. From there he moves to Ramesampeta, travelling 3 kms, which has 135 Mala HHs and collects Rs.2700/—during his stay in September and October. From there he moves to Kotapadu, travelling 5 kms, which has 88 Mala HHs and collects Rs.1760/—@Rs.20 per each HH during his stay in November and December. He reaches where he started off, i.e., Peddapuram by the end of December or the beginning of January, thus completing the circle. His annual net income amounts to Rs. 14,385/-. His movements continue forever like this to eke out his living from the main Mala caste.

Case Study 2 of a Nomadic Family:
The routes in visiting the Main caste Malas (patrons)
in other villages
Diagram 4

Sl.No	Name of the Village	Ammount	Name of the Family Members
1	Vetlapalem	12,000-00	Pathi Ravi-Head (36)
2	Gudaparthi	2,600-00	Pathi Nagamani-Wife (28)
3	Medapadu	2,500-00	Pathi Manga-Daughter (8)
4	Kothuru	2,375-00	Pathi Rambabu-Son (6)
5	Pedabrahmadevam	1,700-00	
6	Hussainpuram	1,560-00	Pathi Sailaja-Daughter (4)
	Total	22,735-00	
	Aata expenditure (deducted)	5,000-00	
	Annual Net Income	17,735-00	

Pathi Ravi and his family stays in Vetlapalem for three months, August, September and October, and collect an amount of Rs. 12,000/—from 200 Mala HHs @20/—per HH and @ 40 per HH toward *'aata'*. From there they move to Gudaparthy, travelling 3 kms by foot, which has 130 Mala HH and collect Rs. 2600 @20 per HH during their stay in November and December.

From there, they move to Medapadu, 3 kms away, which has 125 Mala HH and they collect Rs. 2500/—@ 20 per HH during their stay in January and February. From there they move to Kothuru travelling 5 kms, which has 95 Mala HHs and collect an amount of Rs. 2325 @25 per HH during their stay in March and April.

From Kothuru, they move to Pedabrahmadevam travelling 3 kms which has 85 Mala HH and collect Rs. 1700/-from 85 Mala HH @Rs.20 per HH during their stay in May and June. From there they move to Hussainpuram travelling 5 kms which has 78 Mala HH and collect an amount of Rs.1560/ @Rs. 20 per HH during their stay in July. Travelling 7 kms they reach Vetlapalem, thus completing the circle. The annual net income of this family is Rs. 17,735/—after deducting 'aata' expenses.

CHAPTER V
SUMMARY AND CONCLUSION

Castes in India are ranked endogamous (in-marrying) groups, membership in which is ascribed by birth. There are thousands of castes and sub-castes in India, and each caste is part of a locally based system of interdependence with other groups, involving occupational specialization. Dalits are at the bottom most rungs of the Caste hierarchy. Most of them live outside the main village in the low-lying areas bordering the fields, and are still socially and physically excluded in many villages. Traditionally they are outside the pale of Hinduism but existentially a part and parcel of the village life. Though, things have changed a little now, the Dalits traditionally were not allowed to come into the villages. They were not allowed to see or meet, talk or touch all other caste people. The Hindus idea of 'pollution' kept them away from all other castes as they were considered in a state of 'pollution' all the time for ever. Dalits thus were excluded from the whole Indian Society.

Mala and Madiga are the two prominent Dalit castes in Andhra Pradesh. Though the official word Scheduled Castes include 59 castes, the word Dalit refers mainly to these two castes. Traditionally the Malas are the agricultural Labourers and the Madigas are leather workers. The performance of certain indispensable social, economic and ceremonial tasks integrates them with the village and it's life. The report of the Indian Census 1901, describes the Mala, and Madiga as castes, "who eat beef and pollute even without touch". The origin account of these two castes, Malas and Madigas, establish them as in opposition to each other and this opposition is expressed to the extent of making claims and counter-claims to higher status in the hierarchy. The origin account of Mala Masti clearly establishes their loyalty to the main caste Malas and also the Malas obligation to support the Masti by giving them alms. These rights and obligations bind the Mala Masti and Malas in a permanent relationship of dependence and patronage. It may be noted that the Madigas have their own Madiga Masti.

Mala Masti is a satellite, nomadic, Dalit caste of Andhra Pradesh. They are also known as *Mala Mastin, Mala Masthidi, Mala Machatti* and *Mala Machatollu.* They are known to make visit to the Mala hamlets at regular intervals for their sustenance as collectiong alms is their traditional and primary occupation. They depend exclusively on the main Mala caste for alms and refuse to receive anything from other communities. During harvest times, they entertain the villagers by their songs, dances and spectacular display of acrobatics. The presence of such dependent castes is not limited to Mala caste only. In Andhra Pradesh there are 198 castes and many of them have the dependent castes attached to them. The dependent castes are also addressed as 'Satellite Castes' by some scholars.

In the census reports mention was made of Mala Masti but it was reported that they exist only in three districts in Telangana area. But this study brought to light that they are present in almost all the districts of Andhra Pradesh.

The relationship between the dependent caste and the main caste with reference to the structure and function of these relationships make it into one of a social institution. There are privileges as well as duties impinged on the relationship between the main castes and the dependent castes. But it has to be noted that the dependent relations of these satellite castes are different from the Jajmani and Watandari systems.

The traditional relationship between a main caste and the dependent caste is the committed binding relationship that continues through generations. The dependent castes perform for the sake of their main caste with a sense of commitment but never the same to any other caste. The remuneration they receive is invariably from the main caste but not from others. Here the relationship never ends with receiving of some remuneration for their services. This is a permanent relationship that binds the two parties through the generations.

The Mala Masti are in possession of copper plates on which the Royal decrees are given as to the propriety of the Mala Mastis' right to collect alms from the main caste Mala and the fees prescribed for their acrobatic and power shows. Thus they collect money, grain, clothes, utensils and other goods, getting their marriages done and getting cattle from the main Mala caste. Traditional rights work for the Mala Masti to sustain their lives going around the villages of the patron Mala caste. The benevolent attitude of the main caste is reinforced by the periodic praise singings they receive from the dependent caste.

Singing of the caste lore is an important function of the Dependent castes. The singers of the Dependent caste have created the songs, from the genealogies of the families of the main caste, eulogizing them. This kind of a performance is considered as invaluable by the main caste and the dependent castes as well. The caste lore is thus created in which the emergence of the genealogies of the donor main caste families and their development is praised. As the caste system is built on horizontal and vertical relationships in which all the castes are brought into relationships of superiority and inferiority the main caste draws a sense of pride listening to their caste lore and legends by the dependent castes. In order to dispel the inferiority complex otherwise generated by the caste system these kinds of caste lore work positively. By such of these performances the lowly castes feel that after all they are not that 'lowly'.

The next most important task after the caste lore is to recite genealogical and gotra account. Thus some of the dependent castes have acquired the name of '*gotralavaru*'. The dependent castes visiting their benevolent main caste family goes into a narration of their genealogies and end up with blessing them to prosper more and more in the days to come by. For such an act they receive some payment from the main caste. Their knowledge related to the *gotras* of the Mala caste is one reason why and how their rights over the Mala families are kept intact over generations. Besides, their singing brings to light the appropriateness of their traditional occupation. Their mythological accounts justify the traditional occupation of the main castes and they draw a sense of pride listening to them.

The exhibition of the Mala Mastis' physical prowess and their acrobatic skills in the village provides entertainment and amusement to the large number of villagers who return home at the end of the day after working in the agricultural fields. The *Vipravinodhins* receive alms from the Bramhins by performing magic. It may also be noted here that some of the dependent castes also provide sexual pleasures to the main caste masters.

In turn, the major function of the main caste is to give alms and provide the dependent castes according to the context. It may be noted that the alms are given for the services they provide but not out of compassion or pity. For this reason the dependent castes have the names like, 'caste children', 'caste sons', 'begging children', etc. The royal decrees clearly indicate on the copper plates that they have to be treated as their own children and by giving them alms they have *'punya'* that takes them after death to heaven, otherwise the sin of denying would lead them to condemnation. If any one denies the alms to the dependent caste the caste council of the main caste considers it seriously and the family which refused alms would be made outcaste. The donations made by the main castes are differently called as dowry, begging dowry, *mirasy, sambhavana, vanthan, watan, ilavarasa,* sacrifice, etc.

The Mala Masti social organization is based on the surname groupings and gotras. Those who have the surname *'Nulaka'* belong to the *'Naga'* Gotra and they do not celebrate *Nagula chaviti* and *Deepavali* for a belief that these festivals do not bring any good to them. If they celebrate they may come across any conceivable type of bad event in their lives. This is traditionally believed among them. Those who have *'malisetty'* surname belong to the *'Matsya* (fish) *gotra'* and they do not kill any fish. They indulge in fishing but the fish is killed by others. The Mala Masti of north coastal Andhra region perform *'trimoorty pooja'* (worship of three Hindu gods) and worship *'simhadri appanna'.* In Telangana Area all the Mala Masti belong to only one gotra by name' *Recharla* gotra'.

With regard to their beliefs, if they come across any bad omen they invariably sacrifice a pig. Even on occasions like marriages, changing their residences, caste meetings and other festivals including the life cycle ceremonies they sacrifice a pig. When their belongings drop down to earth from the horse back they consider it as a bad omen. Some parts of the sacrificed pig like the mouth, ears, fat on the neck and the tail are cooked separately without cutting them into pieces. When they have liquor then each piece is broken into smaller ones and eaten. The family with the surname *'malisetti'* takes first the mouth parts as they are the oldest inhabitants. Later, *'the nulaka'* surname family has the right to pick up the ear parts and then the *sikila* and *chikala* families take the neck fat. At the end stand the *kandipalli* family who consume the tail part. They contribute to their caste association by paying some cash to retain this privilege of rights exclusively over their respective parts of the pig. For example, the *malisetti* family pays rupees 30 for the mouth parts; the *nulaka* family 20 rupees for the ears; sikala family divides the neck fat into two parts: *jamula silalu* and *vidi silalu*. The *jamula silalu* are three in number and for which they pay rupees five each and for *vidi silalu* they pay 6 rupees each by the *chikala* family. *Kandipalli* family pays rupees nine to the tail part. With this money they buy liquor together and their own respective parts of the pig.

All economic relations make the Masti to depend solely on the Malas. The Masti consider themselves inferior to Malas. The Malas also maintain the same. Any function celebrated by Mastis is attended invariably by the Malas but the Malas do not partake in the feast hosted by the Mastis except accepting liquor. The raw meat is also accepted but not the cooked dishes. For such occasions the Malas give them rice, tamarind, red-chilly powder over and above what they usually give them. The Mala elders and their women are respected by the Mastis. Others are called by fictitious kin terms.

Their average annual income is reported to be in the range of Rupees 15000-20000, which is barely sufficient for them to make a living. Each and every household in the Malapalli is imposed a fees (*tegam*) which is usually rupees ten by the Mala headman, so that, that money is meant for the 'other' expenses of these Mala Masti. If they perform in the village in addition to this amount another contribution of forty to fifty rupees is paid to them. They collect this money over a period of three to five months to be paid them on the day of performance. If someone in this crowd is impressed by the feats performed by any artiste may announce a presentation of 100 rupees more or less that goes to the artiste only. In addition to this income they grow goats and tend them. They take these goats along with them wherever they go. Occasional fishing also supplements their income. The money thus earned is spent on their marriages, liquor, clothing and other expenses. The one who resides in the villages ask others in other villages to join him on the day of performance so that the collected money is shared among them with the lions share going to the one who invited them. This kind of a mutual cooperation sustains them as a group. Majority of them are engaged as construction labourers. In case of Srikakulam district firewood is collected from the forest and is sold in the nearby market. In S.Kota village many of them are working in the quarry in breaking big boulders. They are all drawing their livelihood from their manual labour.

Every group of surname families has a head man, two members and a *saladu* (messenger). They are elected in annual meetings (*sangham*). Those who are elderly, acceptable and knowledgeable are generally elected. This annual meeting of the surnames association (*sangham)* is usually convened in the month of March every year. All the money matters arrived at in the last meeting have to be settled in this meeting. From this amount a small portion of it is spent toward liquor and the remaining amount is kept with the leaders. The caste association meeting (federation of caste *sangham*) is convened once in every three years and the members are one from each surname *sangham*. This money is deposited to the caste association. One of the main functions of the *sangham* is to advance loans to the needy families and they are required to repay the amount by the next meeting. In case, in the previous meeting arbitration is not agreeable to the members it is presented before the caste association again. Till the dispute is settled irrespective of the time taken for such a purpose the members of the caste association do not leave the place where the meeting is convened.

Most of them are illiterate and a few of them have just reached intermediate as they started sending their children very recently. This is made possible only in case of the settled villages like Korukonda and Singannavalasa.

They worship '*Bethala*' who is '*Anjaneya*' the monkey god. Bethala's sister is *Durgalamma.* Therefore a day before they give performance they enact a drama in which they worship *Durgalamma* by enacting a female role. On the next day they worship *Anjaneya* who is considered as mighty so that they also can perform mighty deeds. On Dasara festival, a pig is sacrificed to *Anjaneya* and *Durgalamma* and the blood is smeared to their instruments like knifes, daggers, shields, drums etc. they break a coconut and worship these two by burning incense. On

Sivarathri day they worship '*Simhadri Appanna*', a local god of Visakhapatnam. All these gods and goddesses are of Hindu religion. A few of them are also found converting into Christianity.

Of late, relations between the Malas and Mala mastis have got strained due to instances of love marriages between these communities which are basically endogamous. With more and more Mala masti turning to settled living from their age old nomadic life, some of them are witnessing definite improvements in their economic and educational status.

From the above account on Mala Masti, the most important point to note is that the system of dependent castes was formed with twin purposes. First of all, its aim is to preserve social identity by differentiating them from other *gotras,* and to perpetuate their genealogies, traditions, ritual behaviour and cultural practices; the second aim is to canvass continuously that their social status is not inferior vis-à-vis other similar castes. In order to accomplish these two tasks the castes have established their own dependent castes. Mala masti is one such satellite dependent caste of the Mala.

NOTES

1. Andhra Pradesh consists of three cultural zones, viz., Andhra, comprising coastal Andhra districts, i.e., Srikakulam, Vizianagaram, Visakhapatnam, East and West Godavari, Krishna, Guntur, Prakasam and Nellore Districts; Rayalaseema comprising Chittor, Cuddapah, Ananthapur, and Kurnool Districts; Telangana comprising Mahabubnagar, Hyderabad, RangaReddy, Medak, Nizamabad, Adilabad, Karimnagar, Warangal, Khammam and Nalgonda districts.

2. Reddy (1952:194) reports that there are 12 endogamous divisions among the Mala. They are: 1. Sarindla; 2.Charu; 3. Reddy bhumi; 4. Pakanati; 5. Pokanati; 6. Rampala; 7. Murikinati; 8. Dayindla; 9. Turasana; 10. Kannada; 11. Koyi; and 12. Rohini. There is no definite number among the Madiga. He, however, notes 5 of them as 1. Gampa Domati; 2. Cheta Dhomati; 3. Teli Dhomati; 4. Vastra Dhomati; and 5. Bhoomi Dhomati. He mentions that these endogamous groups obtain only in Rayalaseema and Nellore districts while in northern *circars* they are not known.

3. Paleru: also called *Jeethagadu*, who is the *Kamin* in *Jajman-Kamin* relationship.

REFERENCES

Ambedkar, B.R.	1948	The Untouchables, Amrit Book Co., Delhi.
Beidelman, T.O.	1959	A Comparative analysis of the Jajmani System. Monograph of the Association for Asian studies, No.8, New York.
Beteille, A.	1966	Caste, Class and Power: Changing patterns of Stratification in a Tanjore Village. Oxford University Press.
_____	1969	Castes: Old and New. Asia Publishing House, Bombay.
Blunt, E.A.H.	1931	The Caste system of Northern India.
Briggs, G.W.	1920	The Chamars. Oxford University Press, London.
Chauhan, B.R.	1967	A Rajasthan Village. Associated Publishing House, New Delhi.
Crooke, W.	1896	Tribes and Castes of the North-West Provinces and Oudh. Office of the Superintendent of Government Press, Calcutta.
Deliege, Robert	1992	Replication and Consensus: Untouchability, Caste and Ideology in India. *Man*, New Series, Vol. 27, No. 1 pp.155-173, Royal Anthropological Institute of Great Britain and Ireland

Dube, S.C.   1955   Indian Village. Routledge and
                                  Kegan Paul, London.

Dumont, Louis.   1980   Homo Hierarchicus: The Caste
                                  System and its Implications.

Dumont, O.L and   1961   Caste, Racism and Stratification:
Pocock   Reflections of a Social
                                  Anthropologist, Contributions to
                                  Indian Sociology, Paris

Fuchs, S.   1949   The Children of Hari: A study
                                  of the Nimar Balahis in Madhya
                                  Pradesh, India. New Order book
                                  Co., Ahmedabad.

Ghurye, G.S.   1961   Caste, Class and Occupation.
                                  Popular Book Depot, Bombay.

Gupta, Dipankar.   2000.   Interrogating Caste:
                                  Understanding Hierarchy and
                                  difference in Indian Society.
                                  Penguin Books, Delhi.

Harper, E.B.   1968   Social consequence of an
                                  'unsuccessful" low caste
                                  movement. In J. Silverberg
                                  (ed), Social Mobility in the
                                  Caste system in India, Mouton
                                  Publisher, The Hague.

Hutton, J.H.   1946   Caste in India. Oxford University
                                  Press, London.

Ibbetson, D.   1916   Punjab Castes, Lahore

Isaacs, H.R   1965   India's Ex-Untouchables, Asia
                                  Publishing House, Bombay.

Iyer, L.A.K   1909   The Cochin Tribes and Castes,
                                  Higginbotham, Madras.

Ketkar, S.   1909   History of Caste in India. Ithaca,
                                  New York.

Leach, E. R.	1960	Aspects of Caste in India, Ceylon and North-West Pakistan. Cambridge University Press, Cambridge
Mayer, A.C.	1960	Caste and Kinship in Central India, Univ, Calif, Press, Berkeley.
McKim Marriot.	1955	Village India. Asia Publishing House, Bombay.
Mendelsohn, Oliver and Marika Vicziany.	1998	*The Untouchables: Subordination, Poverty and the State in Modern India*, Cambridge University Press, New York
Moffat, Michael.	1979	An Untouchable Community in South India: Structure and consensus. Prentice-Hall, New Jersey
Mosse, David.	1994	Idioms of subordination and styles of protest among Christian and Hindu Harijan castes in Tamil Nadu. *Contributions to Indian Sociology* 28(1):67-106.
Naidu, K.S.	2011	Dependence relations of Mala Masti: A Satellite Dalit Cate of Andhra Pradesh. Unpublished Ph.D. Thesis submitted to Andhra University.
Pathak, S.N and Pandey, S.P.	2005	Scheduled Caste Development: A Study of Special Component Plan. Serials Publication, New Delhi.
Panini, M. N.	1996	"The Political Economy of Caste" in 'Caste: It's Twentieth-Century Avatar'. (Ed.) M. N. Srinivas. New Delhi: Viking, 1996.

Prasad, S.K.	1978	Irrigation and Change. Unpublished Ph.D. Thesis submitted to Andhra University.
Rajpramukh, K.E. and P.D.S.Palkumar.	2009	Ambiguous bottom and tacit allegiance: A Satellite Dalit Community of Andhra Pradesh. Man and Life, July-Dec.
Raju, M.V.T.	1980	Persistence and Change: A Study of Watandari System in Rural Telangana with special reference to Medak district. Unpublished Ph.D. thesis submitted to the Dept. of Anthropology, Andhra University
Reddy, N.S.	1952	Transition in Caste Structure in Andhra desh with particular reference to Depressed castes. Unpublished Ph.D. Thesis, Lucknow University.
Risley, H.H.	1915	The People of India. W.Thacker and Co., London.
Sachidananda	1977	The Harijan Elite: A Study of their Status, Networks, Mobility and Role in Transformation. Thomson Press(India) Ltd, Faridabad.
Senart, E.	1930	Caste in India: The facts and the system. Tr.by Sir. E. Denison Ross, Methuen, London.
Singh, T.R.	1969	The Madiga. Ethnographic and Folklore Society, Lucknow.
Sita Deulkar	2004	Dalits: Past, Present and Future. Dominant Publishers, New Delhi.

Srinivas, M.N.	1956	A Note on Sanskritization and Westernization. Far Eastern Quarterly, No.15.
_____	1962	Caste in Modern India and Other Essays. Asia Publishing House, Bombay.
Stevenson, H.N.C.	1954	Status Evaluation in the Hindu Caste System. Journal of the Royal Anthropological Society of Great Britain and Ireland,48,46-57.
Subbachary, P	2000	Caste Myths: Dependent System (in Telugu), Prajashakti Book House, Hyderabad-20.
Subramanyam, Y.S.	1975	Social Change in Village india: An Andhra Case Study. Prithviraj Publisher, New Delhi.
Sudhakarrao, N.	2001	The Structure of South Indian Scheduled Caste: A View. In Dalit Identity and Politics. Sage Pub, New Delhi, Pp.74-96.
Thorat, S	2009	Dalits in India. Sage India, New Delhi
Thurston, E.	1909	Castes and Tribes of Southern India. Govt. Press, Madras
Vincentnathan, L.	1987	*Harijan Sub-culture and Self-Esteem Management in a South Indian Community.* Doctoral dissertation. University of Wisconsin, Madison.
_____	1993a	Untouchable concepts of person and society. *Contributions to Indian Sociology* (n.s.) 27(1):53-82.

| | 1993b | Nanthanar: Untouchable saint and caste Hindu anomaly. Ethos 21(1):154-180. |
| Vincentnathan, S.G. | 1996 | Caste politics, violence, and the panchayat in a South Indian community. *Comparative Studies in Society and History* 38(3):484-509. |

ANNEXURE – I

Table A1.1: Showing Marital Status of Mala Masti at Bheemavaram

Marital Status	Male	% of Total Male	Female	% of Total Female	Total	% of Total Male and Female
Un Married	4	28.6	5	33.3	9	31.0
Married	10	71.4	10	66.7	20	69.0
Widow(er)	0	0.0	0	0.0	0	0.0
Divorced	0	0.0	0	0.0	0	0.0
Total	14	100	15	100	29	100

Table A1.2: Showing Marital Status of Mala Masti at Chepuru

Marital Status	Male	% of Total Male	Female	% of Total Female	Total	% of Total Male and Female
Un Married	5	41.7	4	36.4	9	39.1
Married	7	58.3	7	63.6	14	60.9
Widow(er)	0	0.0	0	0.0	0	0.0
Divorced	0	0.0	0	0.0	0	0.0
Total	12	100	11	100	23	100

Table A1.3: Showing Marital Status of Mala Masti at Gangipalli

Marital Status	Male	% of Total Male	Female	% of Total Female	Total	% of Total Male and Female
Un Married	13	41.9	10	31.2	23	36.5
Married	18	58.1	17	53.1	35	55.6
Widow(er)	0	0.0	5	15.6	5	7.9
Divorced	0	0.0	0	0.0	0	0.0
Total	31	100	32	100	63	100

Table A1.4: Showing Marital Status of
Mala Masti at Gorrekunta

Marital Status	Male	% of Total Male	Female	% of Total Female	Total	% of Total Male and Female
Un Married	12	57.1	12	44.5	24	50.0
Married	11	42.9	10	37.0	19	39.6
Widow(er)	0	0.0	5	18.5	5	10.4
Divorced	0	0.0	0	0.0	0	0.0
Total	23	100	27	100	50	100

Table A1.5: Showing Marital Status of
Mala Masti at Nalluru

Marital Status	Male	% of Total Male	Female	% of Total Female	Total	% of Total Male and Female
Un Married	5	26.3	7	33.3	12	30.0
Married	14	73.7	14	66.7	28	70.0
Widow(er)	0	0.0	0	0.0	0	0.0
Divorced	0	0.0	0	0.0	0	0.0
Total	19	100	21	100	40	100

Table A1.6: Showing Marital Status of
Mala Masti at Singannavalasa

Marital Status	Male	% of Total Male	Female	% of Total Female	Total	% of Total Male and Female
Un Married	20	40.0	16	32.7	36	36.4
Married	28	56.0	27	55.1	55	55.6
Widow(er)	1	2.0	6	12.2	7	7.1
Divorced	1	2.0	0	0.0	1	1.0
Total	50	100	49	100	99	100

Table A1.7: Showing Marital Status of
Mala Masti at Paleru

Marital Status	Male	% of Total Male	Female	% of Total Female	Total	% of Total Male and Female
Un Married	15	60.0	3	20.0	18	45.0
Married	10	40.0	10	66.7	20	50.0
Widow(er)	0	0.0	2	13.3	2	5.0
Divorced	0	0.0	0	0.0	0	0.0
Total	25	100	15	100	40	100

Table A1.8: Showing Marital Status of
Mala Masti at Rangapuram

Marital Status	Male	% of Total Male	Female	% of Total Female	Total	% of Total Male and Female
Un Married	7	53.8	3	27.3	10	41.7
Married	6	46.2	6	54.5	12	50.0
Widow(er)	0	0.0	2	18.2	2	8.3
Divorced	0	0.0	0	0.0	0	0.0
Total	13	100	11	100	24	100

Table A1.9: Showing Marital Status of
Mala Masti at Samalkot

Marital Status	Male	% of Total Male	Female	% of Total Female	Total	% of Total Male and Female
Un Married	11	45.8	7	29.2	18	37.5
Married	12	50.0	13	54.2	25	52.1
Widow(er)	0	0.0	2	8.3	2	4.2
Divorced	1	4.2	2	8.3	3	6.2
Total	24	100	24	100	48	100

Table A1.10: Showing Marital Status of
Mala Masti at Sayampalem

Marital Status	Male	% of Total Male	Female	% of Total Female	Total	% of Total Male and Female
Un Married	17	44.7	16	41.0	33	42.9
Married	19	50.0	19	48.7	38	49.4
Widow(er)	1	2.6	2	5.1	3	3.9
Divorced	1	2.6	2	5.1	3	3.9
Total	38	100	39	100	77	100

Table A1.11: Showing Marital Status of
Mala Masti at West Gonagudem

Marital Status	Male	% of Total Male	Female	% of Total Female	Total	% of Total Male and Female
Married	55	41.98	53	49.07	108	45.19
Unmarried	64	48.85	41	37.96	105	43.93
Widow(er)	3	2.29	4	3.70	7	2.93
Unavailable data	9	6.87	10	9.26	19	7.95
Total	131	100	108	100	239	100

Table A1.12: Showing Marital Status of
Mala Masti at Gollapet

Marital Status	Male	% of Total Male	Female	% of Total Female	Total	% of Total Male and Female
Married	12	53.8	12	38.7	24	42.1
Unmarried	14	46.2	11	35.5	25	43.9
Widow(er)	0	0.0	7	22.6	7	12.3
Divorced	0	0.0	1	3.2	1	1.8
Total	26	100	31	100	57	100

Table A1.13: Showing Marital Status of
Mala Masti at Chodavaram

Marital Status	Male	% of Total Male	Female	% of Total Female	Total	% of Total Male and Female
Married	18	48.60	17	58.65	35	53.03
Unmarried	19	51.40	9	31.00	28	42.42
Widow(er)	0	0.00	3	10.35	3	4.55
Divorced	0	0	0	0	0	0
Total	37	100	29	100	66	100

Table A1.14: Showing Marital Status of
Mala Masti at S.Kota

Marital Status	Male	% of Total Male	Female	% of Total Female	Total	% of Total Male and Female
Married	32	54.24	32	62.75	64	58.18
Unmarried	26	44.07	17	33.33	43	39.09
Widow(er)	0	0.00	2	3.92	2	1.82
Divorced	1	1.69	0	0.00	1	0.91
Total	59	100	51	100	110	100

ANNEXURE – II

Table A2.1: Showing occupational distribution of Mala Masti in Palakonda

Primary Occupation	Total	% of Total	Secondary Occupation	Total	% of Total
Un-skilled Worker	12	12.2	Masonry	2	2.0
Labourer	38	37.8	Fire wood Collection	12	11.2
House Wife	23	23.5	Labourer	12	12.2
Caste occupation	5	5.1	Painting	1	1.0
Conductor	1	1.0	Unskilled Worker	72	73.6
Private Job	2	2.0			
Student	18	18.4			
Total	**99**	**100**		**99**	**100**

Table A2.2: Showing occupational distribution of Mala Masti in Samarlakota

Primary Occupation	Total	% of Total	Secondary Occupation	Total	% of Total
Un-skilled Worker	7	14.6	Un-skilled Worker	37	77.1
Labourer	24	50.0	Labourer	10	20.8
House Wife	9	18.8	House Wife	1	2.1
Student	7	14.6			
Rickshaw Puller	1	2.1			
Total	**48**	**100**		**48**	**100**

Table A2.3: Showing occupational distribution of Mala Masti in Syampalem

Primary Occupation	Total	% of Total	Secondary Occupation	Total	% of Total
Un-skilled worker	6	7.8	Un-skilled worker	59	76.6
Labourer	29	37.6	Labourer	16	20.8
House Wife	17	22.1	Caste occupation	1	1.3
Student	18	23.4	Paleru	1	1.3
Paleru[3]	7	9.1			
Total	**77**	**100**		**77**	**100**

Table A2.4: Showing occupational distribution of Mala Masti in Paleru

Primary Occupation	Total	% of Total	Secondary Occupation	Total	% of Total
Auto Driver	2	5.0	Un-skilled worker	24	60.0
Labourer	13	32.5	Labourer	10	25.0
House Wife	10	25.0	Agri gold Agent	1	2.5
Student	13	32.5	Fishing	2	5.0
Caste occupation	1	2.5	Stiching	1	2.5
Stiching	1	2.5	Vegetable Venders	2	5.0
Total	**40**	**100**		**40**	**100**

Table A2.5: Showing occupational distribution of Mala Masti in Bhimavaram

Primary Occupation	Total	% of Total	Secondary Occupation	Total	% of Total
Un-skilled worker	1	3.4	Un-skilled worker	19	65.5
House Wife	10	34.6	Labourer	10	34.5
Labourer	9	31.0			
Lorry Driver	1	3.4			
Students	8	27.6			
Total	**29**	**100**		**29**	**100**

Table A2.6: Showing occupational distribution of Mala Masti in Gorrekunta

Primary Occupation	Total	% of Total	Secondary Occupation	Total	% of Total
Driver	2	2.7	Agriculture Labourer	10	13.5
Govt. Employee	1	1.4	Un-skilled worker	64	86.5
Caste occupation	4	5.4			
House Wife	9	12.2			
Labourer	21	28.4			
Private Job	2	2.7			
Retired Employee	1	1.4			
Students	27	36.5			
Un-skilled worker	7	9.5			
Total	**74**	**100**		**74**	**100**

Table A2.7: Showing occupational distribution of Mala Masti in Gangipalli

Primary Occupation	Total	% of Total	Secondary Occupation	Total	% of Total
Caste occupation	9	14.3	Caste occupation	1	1.6
Un-skilled workers	6	9.5	Un-skilled workers	46	73.0
House Wife	12	19.0	Agricultural Labourer	16	25.4
Students	15	23.8			
Labourer	2	3.2			
Agricultural Labourer	17	27.0			
Govt. Employee	1	1.6			
Private Employee	1	1.6			
Total	**63**	**100**		**63**	**100**

Table A2.8: Showing occupational distribution of
Mala Masti in Chepuru

Primary Occupation	Total	% of Total	Secondary Occupation	Total	% of Total
Agricultural Labourer	16	24.7	Ag. Labourer	4	6.2
Beedi making	2	3.1	Beedi making	16	24.6
Driver	1	1.5	Un-skilled workers	45	69.2
Working in Gulf countries	8	12.3			
House Wife	21	32.3			
Un-skilled workers	7	10.8			
Students	9	13.8			
Teacher	1	1.5			
Total	**65**	**100**		**65**	**100**

Table A2.9: Showing occupational distribution of
Mala Masti in Gollapeta

Primary Occupation	Total	% of Total	Secondary Occupation	Total	% of Total
Un-skilled worker	4	7.0	Agricultural Labourers	40	70.2
Gulf/ Beedi Making	4	7.0	Beedi Making	4	7.0
House Wife	14	24.6		0	0.0
Labourer	19	33.3	Labourer	13	22.8
Nurse	1	1.8		0	0.0
Students	15	26.3		0	0.0
Total	**57**	**100**		**57**	**100**

Table A2.10: Showing occupational distribution of Mala Masti in West Gonegudem

Primary Occupation	Total	% of Total	Secondary Occupation	Total	% of Total
Un-skilled workers	100	41.8	Un-skilled workers	164	68.6
Labourer	62	25.9	Labourer	45	18.8
Caste Occupation	6	2.5	House Wife	30	12.6
Private Employee	4	1.7			
House Wife	34	14.2			
Students	31	13.0			
Fruit venders	2	0.8			
Total	**239**	**100**		**239**	**100**

Table A2.11: Showing occupational distribution of Mala Masti in Chodavaram

Primary Occupation	Total	% of Total	Secondary Occupation	Total	% of Total
Un-skilled worker	10	15.2	Un-skilled worker	46	69.7
House Wife	10	15.2	Labourer	20	30.3
Labourer	32	48.5			
Caste occupation	6	9.1			
Students	8	12.1			
Total	**66**	**100**		**66**	**100**

Table A2.12: Showing occupational distribution of Mala Masti in Srungavarapukota

Primary Occupation	Total	% of Total	Secondary Occupation	Total	% of Total
Un-skilled workers	29	26.4	Un-skilled workers	87	79.1
Labourer	45	40.9	Labourer	15	13.6
Caste occupation	1	0.9	House Wife	8	7.3
Private Employee	2	1.8			
House Wife	20	18.2			
Students	12	10.9			
Fruit venders	1	0.9			
Total	**110**	**100**		**110**	**100**

ANNEXURE – III

Table A3.1: Showing Educational Status of Mala Masti in Singannavalasa Village

Level of Education	Male	% of Total Male	Female	% of Total Female	Total	% of Total Male and Female
Illiterate	11	22.0	24	49.0	35	35.4
Primary	13	26.0	13	26.5	26	26.5
Secondary	16	32.0	12	24.5	28	28.3
Intermediate	5	10.0	0	0.0	5	5.1
Degree	5	10.0	0	0.0	5	5.1
Total	**50**	**100**	**49**	**100**	**99**	**100**

Table A3.2: Showing Educational Status of Mala Masti in Samalkot Village

Level of Education	Male	% of Total Male	Female	% of Total Female	Total	% of Total Male and Female
Illiterate	16	66.7	19	79.2	35	72.9
Primary	8	33.3	2	8.3	10	20.8
Secondary	0	0.0	3	12.5	3	6.3
Intermediate	0	0.0	0	0.0	0	0.0
Degree	0	0.0	0	0.0	0	0.0
Total	**24**	**100**	**24**	**100**	**48**	**100**

Table A3.3: Showing Educational Status of Mala Masti in Sayampalem Village

Level of Education	Male	% of Total Male	Female	% of Total Female	Total	% of Total Male and Female
Illiterate	25	65.8	25	64.1	50	64.9
Primary	9	23.7	11	28.2	20	26.0
Secondary	3	7.9	3	7.7	6	7.8
Intermediate	1	2.6	0	0.0	1	1.3
Degree	0	0.0	0	0.0	0	0.0
Total	**38**	**100**	**39**	**100**	**77**	**100**

Table A3.4: Showing Educational Status of Mala Masti in Paleru Village

Level of Education	Male	% of Total Male	Female	% of Total Female	Total	% of Total Male and Female
Illiterate	2	8.0	10	66.7	12	30.0
Primary	8	32.0	3	20.0	11	27.5
Secondary	9	36.0	1	6.7	10	25.0
Intermediate	1	4.0	1	6.7	2	5.0
Anganwadi	1	4.0	0	0.0	1	2.5
Degree	2	8.0	0	0.0	2	5.0
B.A., B.Ed.	2	8.0	0	0.0	2	5.0
Total	**25**	**100**	**15**	**100**	**40**	**100**

Table A3.5: Showing Educational Status of Mala Masti in Pamarru Village

Level of Education	Male	% of Total Male	Female	% of Total Female	Total	% of Total Male and Female
Illiterate	12	14.1	41	45.1	53	30.1
Primary	34	40.0	12	13.2	46	26.1
Secondary	28	32.9	24	26.4	52	29.5
Intermediate	1	1.2	3	3.3	4	2.3
Anganwadi	7	8.2	11	12.1	18	10.2
Degree	2	2.4	0	0.0	2	1.1
ITI	1	1.2	0	0.0	1	0.6
Total	**85**	**100**	**91**	**100**	**176**	**100**

Table A3.6: Showing Educational Status of Mala Masti in BheemavaramVillage

Level of Education	Male	% of Total Male	Female	% of Total Female	Total	% of Total Male and Female
Illiterate	7	50.0	11	73.3	18	46.2
Primary	4	28.6	1	6.7	5	12.8
Secondary	1	7.1	1	6.7	2	5.1
Intermediate	0	0.0	2	13.3	2	5.1
Anganwadi Students	2	14.3	0	0.0	2	5.1
Total	**14**	**100**	**15**	**100**	**29**	**100**

Table A3.7: Showing Educational Status of Mala Masti in GorrekuntaVillage

Level of Education	Male	% of Total Male	Female	% of Total Female	Total	% of Total Male and Female
Illiterate	6	16.7	20	52.6	26	31.0
Primary	8	22.2	6	15.8	14	16.7
Secondary	16	44.4	10	26.3	26	31.0
Intermediate	4	11.1	2	5.3	6	7.1
Degree	2	5.6	0	0.0	2	2.4
Total	**36**	**100**	**38**	**100**	**74**	**100**

Table A3.8: Showing Educational Status of Mala Masti in Gangipalli Village

Level of Education	Male	% of Total Male	Female	% of Total Female	Total	% of Total Male and Female
Illiterate	12	38.7	22	67.7	34	53.2
Primary	7	22.6	3	9.7	10	16.1
Secondary	8	25.8	7	22.6	15	24.2
Intermediate	1	3.2	0	0.0	1	1.6
M.A.B.Ed.	1	3.2	0	0.0	1	1.6
Anganwadi Students	2	6.5	0	0.0	2	3.2
Total	**31**	**100**	**31**	**100**	**63**	**100**

Table A3.9: Showing Educational Status of Mala Masti in Chepuru Village

Level of Education	Male	% of Total Male	Female	% of Total Female	Total	% of Total Male and Female
Illiterate	9	29.0	14	43.8	23	36.5
Primary	3	9.7	3	9.4	6	9.5
Secondary	12	38.7	8	25.0	20	31.7
Intermediate	4	12.9	7	21.9	11	17.5
Degree	2	6.5	0	0.0	2	3.2
B.A.B.Ed.	1	3.2	0	0.0	1	1.6
Total	**31**	**100**	**32**	**100**	**63**	**100**

Table A3.10: Showing Educational Status of Mala Masti in S. Kota Village

Level of Education	Male	% of total Male	Female	% of total female	Total	% of total male and female
Illiterates	27	45.76	29	56.86	56	50.91
Primary	15	25.42	6	11.76	21	19.09
Secondary	13	22.03	13	25.49	26	23.64
Inter	1	1.69	2	3.92	3	2.73
Degree	3	5.08	1	1.96	4	3.64
PG	0	0.00	0	0.00	0	0.00
Total	**59**	**100**	**51**	**100**	**110**	**100**

Table A3.11: Showing Educational Status of Mala Masti in Chodavaram Village

Level of Education	Male	% of total Male	Female	% of total Female	Total	% of total male and female
Illiterates	21	56.76	16	55.17	37	56.06
Primary	6	16.22	5	17.24	11	16.67
Secondary	6	16.22	5	17.24	11	16.67
Inter	3	8.11	1	3.45	4	6.06
Degree	1	2.70	0	0.00	1	1.52
PG	0	0.00	1	3.45	1	1.52
Nursing	0	0.00	1	3.45	1	1.52
Total	**37**	**100**	**29**	**100**	**66**	**100**

Table A3.12: Showing Educational Status of Mala Masti in West Gonagudem Village

Level of Education	Male	% of total Male	Female	% of total Female	Total	% of total male and female
Illiterates	92	70.23	72	66.67	164	68.62
Primary	21	16.03	16	14.81	37	15.48
Secondary	5	3.82	8	7.41	13	5.44
Inter	3	2.29	2	1.85	5	2.09
Degree	1	0.76	0	0.00	1	0.42
PG	0	0.00	0	0.00	0	0.00
Unavailable Data	9	6.87	10	9.26	19	7.95
Total	**131**	**100**	**108**	**100**	**239**	**100**

Table A3.13: Showing Educational Status of
Mala Masti in Gollapet Village

Level of Education	Male	% of total male	Female	% of total female	Total	% of total male and female
Illiterates	5	19.2	16	51.6	21	36.8
Primary	8	30.8	6	19.4	14	24.6
Secondary	7	26.9	6	19.4	13	22.8
Inter	5	19.3	2	6.5	7	12.3
Degree	1	3.8	1	3.2	2	3.5
Total	**26**	**100**	**31**	**100**	**57**	**100**